# CHILI PEPPER

## Moments of Spicy Passion

WHITE STAR PUBLISHERS

Photography by
**FABIO PETRONI**

Text by
**CINZIA TRENCHI**

Prefaces:
ENZO MONACO
President of the Italian Chili Pepper Academy
www.peperoncino.org

MARIO DADOMO
Azienda Agraria Sperimentale STUARD
www.stuard.it

Graphic design
CLARA ZANOTTI

Food Stylist
FRANCESCA BAGNASCHI

# contents

# TWO WORLDS MEET
## ADDING FLAVOR TO THE KITCHEN

The chili pepper came to Europe with the voyages of Christopher Columbus and the discovery of America, arriving first in Spain, in Palos in 1493, and then Italy. To better understand those years, however, we have to take a step back in time to see the climate of the fifteenth century.

That era was strongly dominated by a crisis in the spice trade, a crisis of exceptional magnitude, which, in many ways, is comparable to the energy crisis of the twentieth century: if today's dwindling, finite resource is oil, back then, it was spices.

From the twelfth to the fifteenth century, the spice trade was of vital importance to Europe in economic terms. Venice, at the time, was the industry's main hub and the period of maximum prosperity for the city coincided with that of the highest consumption of black pepper in Europe. With the revenue from this trade, Venetian merchants built their famed marble palaces: the sumptuous Venetian architecture still serving as a monument to the spice trade and the wealth it generated.

This would not last, however, and there were three main reasons for the fifteenth century spice trade crisis: a growth in demand, transport difficulties and the increase of customs and duties.

Demand had increased with the increasing wealth of the bourgeoisie, who had begun to imitate the nobility. The desire of this group to flaunt their newfound wealth led to an increase in the demand for spices, which at that time were a real status symbol for the noble classes. With the goods now being moved in increasing numbers, the traditional spice road, which had allowed trade for centuries, was now old and inadequate. The route involved crossing the Indian Ocean in Syria, through the Isthmus of Suez, Alexandria, Egypt. Goods would then be brought by sea to Venice, eventually crossing the Alps by land to reach the markets of central and northern Europe. Aside from increased demand, the Mamluks in Egypt and the Turks in Asia Minor, also limited the freedom of trade and imposed very high taxes. For these reasons, the cost of spices grew exponentially. Lorenzo the Magnificent, prince and writer, reported that the price of a nutmeg was equivalent to that of two oxen.

From this crisis came the feverish search for a cheaper trade route, one that could circumvent trade barriers and transport larger quantities of goods and possibly even new spices. Finding a new route to the Indies became something of an obsession in the fifteenth century, and an entire generation took up the search. This climate provided the backdrop for the voyages of Christopher Columbus and Vasco da Gama.

It was during his first voyage, in fact, that Columbus "discovered" the chili pepper. Arriving in Hispaniola, modern day Haiti, he wrote in his travel log, dated January 15, 1493: "There is plenty of pure aji, which is their pepper, and it is of a quality that far surpasses black pepper. There is no one that eats without it as they deem it very healing."

This became the basis for the chili pepper's European sale pitch: a new spice, better than black pepper, that was good for your health. Sensing its potential, Columbus immediately brought the chili pepper to the Spanish court, certain he had a potentially big business in his hands. In fact, during the second trip, in 1494, his team, led by the ship's doctor Diego Alvarez Chanca, began cultivation. Sixty years later, the chili pepper had spread throughout Spain, as evidenced by writings of Bartolomé de Las Casas, which date back to 1552.

From Spain, the chili pepper would eventually spread to Italy and the rest of the Old World. In 1568, famed famous botanist Pier Andrea Mattioli gave a precise description of it in his writings, calling it the "pepper of India". It must be said, however, that the chili pepper failed to live up to expectations, at least in an economic sense. This was down to two reasons: it wasn't embraced by the rich and noble classes, who did not appreciate its spicy flavor; and the plant's easy cultivation (it can grow in a vase) eliminated the need for travel and trade with its land of origin.

The so-called "pepper of India", therefore, seemed destined to a humble fate, never replacing Oriental spices in the cuisine of the upper classes. However, it soon was taken up by the poorer classes, who saw its potential as a condiment, both for bland food and for vegetable-based dishes, which may have been considered less refined than the foods of the wealthy.

In time, it would be used in baking or to accompany other products of American origin, including eggplants, tomatoes and potatoes, becoming, in the process, the "spice of the poor." All it took was a bit of creativity and imagination, and peppers were ready for a starring role in original dishes around the world.

**Enzo Monaco**

*President*
*Italian Chili Pepper Academy*
*e.monaco@peperoncino.org*

# SPICY PLEASURE

## BY CINZIA TRENCHI

Try to imagine the world without the chili pepper. Remove it from Mexico, Italy, Spain, Africa, the Caribbean, Texas, Indonesia and nearly a quarter of the world's cuisines that make ample use of it. Eliminate the color it gives dishes, and for a moment, imagine the kitchen in black and white!

What would become of the classic Italian spaghetti based exclusively on oil, garlic and chili peppers? And what about Indian fruit chutney? The textures may stay the same, but they would lack the provocative spiciness that make these dishes irresistible.

When Columbus first brought it back from "India" (which of course turned out to be America), he hoped the chili pepper would be used to replace spices that were already well known. However, given the pepper's adaptability and simple cultivation, and the fact that the upper classes did not take to its flavor, it remained relegated to the most humble kitchens, spreading slowly (and reaching its potential) over time.

The word "chili" refers to the spicy variety of Capsicum plants, which range from all shades of light yellow to orange, red, green, and a brown that's nearly black. Many botanists are fans of the chili pepper, and every year, new colors and shapes are added to the variety available worldwide. But with regards to our approach to the chili in the kitchen, what do we need to know to get closer to this wonderful ingredient and prepare many delicious recipes?

The kitchen is an immense source of discovery, with local flavors and aromas providing deep, often unexpected connections to other times, places and emotions. The aim of this collection is to tell, through these spicy recipes, how deeply rooted the chili pepper is in the culinary traditions of much of the world. Think of it as a small journey through flavors, colors and culinary delights, ranging from one continent to another, a collection of recipes that strives to add to our wealth of knowledge about food, the sharing of tastes and occasionally unusual combinations. The book includes six chapters from which to draw inspiration, for appetizers, first courses, main courses, side dishes, sauces and desserts.

Our journey touches distant countries: with the harissa, the exquisite and powerful red sauce typical of northern Africa, we enliven meat and couscous dishes; with the chili pepper, we rekin-

dle the fire of Mexican beans, seasoning them with some of the hottest chilies in the world; from India, arguably the real home of the beloved Capsicum, we take the amazing tandoori chicken, with all its tantalizing and appetizing aromas; from the Italian tradition, we draw inspiration for creative pasta seasonings, both simple and rich, but always caressed by that underlining spice; with ceviche, finally, we come to our star's place of origin, with sunny yellow peppers, and barely perceptible aroma, rich in nuances. There are, of course, many other tasty suggestions and recipes in this collection, some complex, some easy and quick to prepare.

Here is a recommendation suitable for all recipes: though chili peppers range from midly spicy to very hot, it is better to approach them caution. Once they have become part of your eating and cooking habits, however, even the most powerful can be regular ingredients for delicious dishes. But before that happens, we recommend extreme care when handling their fiery character!

At this point the question is, why does the chili pepper get so much attention? How is it possible that it has insinuated itself so deeply in so many different regional cuisines? How can that be possible, considering how spicy some of these peppers are (so spicy, in fact, just eating them can sometimes be seen as a challenge)?

Technically, the main reason is that capsaicin (or capseicina) contained in the pepper acts as a drug.

This alkaloid stimulates the production of endorphins in the brain to quench the scorching heat perceived by the mucous membranes. For this reason, the "pain" involved derives great pleasure! The chili is also a powerful antibacterial (which is why it is consumed most especially in hot countries), helping to maintain thermal equilibrium. It is rich in vitamins and minerals and stimulates fat metabolism.

There are many virtues of this pepper, feared, loved and appreciated by many, not only as a spice but as a true partner in the kitchen, enriching the color and verve of everyday dishes—adding a touch of vivaciousness and pleasure to simple salads, pastas, and even chocolate desserts—in a triumph of unexpected, suggestive flavor.

# A WORLD OF COLOR WITH THE CHILI PEPPER

BY MARIO DADOMO

The cultivated chili pepper mainly pertains to 5 species.

Capsicum annuum, to which many of the varieties commonly grown belong, including sweet peppers (this species also includes the great majority of varieties used mainly for ornamental purposes)

Capsicum baccatum, which includes the aji amarillo and other South American varieties

Capsicum chinense, which includes the habanero and others; these peppers are among the absolute hottest

Capsicum frutescens, which includes some types of Tabasco

Capsicum pubescens, which, with hairy leaves and black seeds, is the most unique species.

Another twenty or so wild species have been documented; although they're fascinating from a botanical perspective, they're not available commercially, so outside the scope of our discussion here.

Growing chili peppers is quite simple and one of the reasons why it has spread around the globe. What matters primarily is being able to make use of light and heat for a sufficiently long period of time, as well as the availability of adequate water intake.

In Europe, seeds are usually sowed in a heated greenhouse (or other protected environments) from January to March, and then transplanted outdoors from April to June, when temperatures are optimal. This allows the plant to complete its growing cycle and production before the next period of frost. None of the varieties currently grown, in fact, bear the cold, and all are designed to fail if not properly protected. Whoever wants to keep the plants for the following year, therefore, should grow them in pots and protect them from the frost, placing them in front of an appropriate light source, before the temperature drops to near freezing. In sub-tropical and tropical areas, the chili pepper can be grown almost all year round. In the southern hemisphere, the process is similar to that suggested for Europe, but of course the seasons are reversed.

With regards to the land, the chili adapts to many different situations, both in terms of structure, composition and pH, even if, like most other vegetables, it prefers a medium soil mixture, well-structured and doted with appropriate organic matter, and a generally neutral reaction. Rotation is important to avoid soil fatigue and the development of pests and weeds, among other things. Alternating ensures that chili peppers and other Solanaceae turn out best, with plants only returning to the same

plot after 3 to 4 years. The nutritional requirements are not particularly relevant for survival, but proper development should involve the elements of fertility required for a nutritional balance.

In a nutshell, you need nitrogen (especially in a pot, as irrigation causes a continuous washing out), phosphorus and potassium, according to the needs of the crop, soil type, and so forth; other elements may be required in special cases. Irrigation is important and you should never allow the substrate to dry out, although you can still make up for a temporary wilting of the foliage with timely irrigation.

In phytosanitary terms, we can safely say that the chili is usually much more rustic than the different varieties of sweet pepper, and phenomena of *Phytophthora capsici* are unlikely to occur. In this short space, and without a comprehensive and thorough examination, it's best to pay attention to bacteria (contained with copper salts), viruses (removing infected plants is required), tracheomycosis (also in this case infected plants have to be sacrificed) and any pests (aphids, mites etc..) which are fought, if necessary, with specific products.

There is a great natural biodiversity, but the ease of creating new varieties by crossing and selection has stimulated the creation of thousands around the world (at the field catalog of the Agrarian Experimental Stuard in Parma, Italy, there are already more than 500, including over 400 newly created).

From the iconography of this volume, the large variety of colors  when these peppers are fully ripe (includine red, yellow, orange, brown and more) are already clear, to say nothing of the color changes that occur during the ripening period (green, straw-color, a blackish hue, and purple), and the range of colors that can be simultaneously present on the same plant.

We take this opportunity to remind you that all varieties of chili peppers are edible and those who come to full maturity are generally richer in flavor.

Genetic variability affects not only the color but also the size of the pepper (from those that look like a pinhead to those over 30 cm long), shape (elongated, conical, round, pear-shaped, "bell" and so on) and the degree of hotness (from completely sweet to very high levels of hotness). These are in addition to the variability in leaf color (different intensities of green, blackish, variegated) and flowers (whitish, greenish or purple, or variegated with yellow spots) as well as in the behavior and development of the plant, as illustrated on the following pages.

**ABBRACCIO**
*Capsicum annuum*
Medium-high heat

An Italian variety, harvested in bunches ("Abbraccio" means "hug")

**ACI SIVRI**
*Capsicum annuum*
Mild to medium

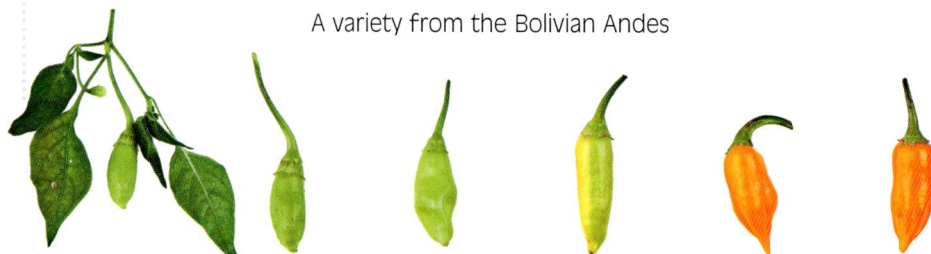

A variety from Turkey

**ACRATA**
*Capsicum annuum*
Hot

A variety native to South America

**ACROBAT**
*Capsicum annuum*
Hot

Leaves are less hairy than the Acrata

**AGATHA**
*Capsicum annuum*
Medium

A variety noted for its bright yellow color

**AJI COLORADO**
*Capsicum baccatum*
Mild to medium

A variety from the Bolivian Andes

**AJI HABANERO**
*Capsicum baccatum*
Mild to medium

A variety from South America

A pleasant variety in both taste and appearance

**ALFIERE**
*Capsicum annuum*
Mild to medium

A pleasant variety in both taste and appearance

**ALI**
*Capsicum annuum*
Medium to hot

A sweet pepper

**AMAZON CHILI ROMA**
*Capsicum chinense*
Sweet

A pepper with a beautiful bright orange color

**AMIGA**
*Capsicum annuum*
Medium to hot

A colorful pepper that's also suitable for ornamental growth

**ANDA**
*Capsicum annuum*
Medium to hot

A variety from the country of the same name

**AZERBAIJAN**
*Capsicum annuum*
Mild to medium

Unripe peppers look like bunches of grapes

**BACCO 1**
*Capsicum annuum*
Medium

## BASSOTTO
*Capsicum annuum*
Medium

Round peppers, harvested in bunches

## BEBEBÈ
*Capsicum annuum*
Medium

An orange pepper that's also suitable for ornamental growth

## BELVIOLA
*Capsicum annuum*
Mild to medium

Immature peppers have a lively purple color

## BESLER'S CHERRY
*Capsicum annuum*
Medium to hot

An ancient variety described as early as 1613

## BIG JIM
*Capsicum annuum*
Mild

A variety from New Mexico with very large fruits

## BODYGUARD
*Capsicum annuum*
Medium to hot

A hybrid, with fruits that go from blackish to red

## BRITISH
*Capsicum annuum*
Mild

A variety that bears aromatic, fleshy, rounded peppers

A variety from Indonesia

Colored fruits with an unusual shape

A variety from Bolivia

A typical cone-shaped chili pepper

A variety from Brazil

A variety from Mexico with brown fruit

A pleasant variety in both taste and appearance with blackish leaves

**DADDY**
*Capsicum annuum*
Medium

A pleasant variety in both taste and appearance

**DELICATE**
*Capsicum annuum*
Mild

This plant bears rounded fruits

**DOLCEVITA**
*Capsicum annuum*
Sweet

A pleasant variety in both taste and appearance

**DUE MORI**
*Capsicum annuum*
Mild to medium

Fruits are harvested in bunches; also a good ornamental plant

**FATAL**
*Capsicum chinense*
Very hot

A variety from central Africa

**FRIARIELLO**
*Capsicum annuum*
Sweet

This variety is also known as "friariello"

**FUEGUITOS**
*Capsicum annuum*
Medium

Fruits are harvested in bunches; also a good ornamental plant

A variety from Mexico

**GUAJILLO**
*Capsicum annuum*
Very mild

A variety from Mexico

**ORANGE HABANERO**
*Capsicum chinense*
Very hot

A variety of habanero with dark fruit

**CHOCOLATE
HABANERO**
*Capsicum chinense*
Very hot

A variety of habanero with red fruit

**RED SAVINA
HABANERO**
*Capsicum chinense*
Very hot

A variety of habanero with red fruit

**RED HABAÑERO**
*Capsicum chinense*
Very hot

The variety used for the famous red sauce

**HARISSA**
*Capsicum annuum*
Mild to medium

A variety from Calabria, Italy

**IDEALINO**
*Capsicum annuum*
Medium

17

**INDIANO**
*Capsicum annuum*
Medium

A variety from India

**JALAPEÑO**
*Capsicum annuum*
Medium

Originally from Mexico, this is the most consumed chili pepper in the U.S.

**NAGA MORICH**
*Capsicum chinense*
Extremely hot

This Indian variety is one of the hottest in the world

**SALAMANDRA**
*Capsicum annuum*
Medium

Fruits are harvested in bunches; also a good ornamental plant

**SCOZZESE**
*Capsicum annuum*
Low-medium spiciness

This variety is very similar to the Scotch Bonnet pepper

**SUAVITO**
*Capsicum annuum*
Mild to medium

Miniature peppers

**TABASCO**
*Capsicum frutescens*
Hot

The peppers used for the famous sauce

A variety from Thailand

**THAI**
*Capsicum annuum*
Very hot

Elongated fruits

**VIGEI**
*Capsicum annuum*
Mild to medium

Brightly colored fruits

**YEBO**
*Capsicum annuum*
Very mild

# APPETIZERS

Our journey into the spicy world of the chili pepper begins with a selection of irreplaceable starters, in which the chili pepper is not only an ingredient, but the ingredient par excellence, one that often ties that recipe to a specific location. In that way, we set off for North Africa with harissa for bread bouzgene, ideal to enjoy with tomato sauces and condiments; we consult with the Italian tradition to prepare magnificent mussels, the taste of the sea alternating with the robust spiciness of the idealino; we prepare ceviche with the conquistador, perfect for combining the freshness of lime, the aroma of cilantro and the flavor of the fish!

It hasn't always been easy to find the perfect pepper, though as its use has become more widespread, more exotic varieties can now be found – dried, ground or powdered – in your local supermarket. Specialty and ethnic groceries usually offer an interesting variety of fresh chili peppers, and some (harissa, habanero or idealino, for example) are even available as creams, ready to be added to sauces.

The chili pepper is not always spicy. This is the case of the Italian friariello, a tasty Capsicum with a bright green color, firm texture and an outstanding, sweet flavor, ideal for cooking tasty omelet's. The same can certainly not be said about the yellow South American aji habanero, with which you can prepare a crispy tempura, with an impressive degree of spiciness.

To try stuffing peppers with tuna, the British or delicate pepper variety are recommended, as both are fleshy, characterized by a firm texture and just a slight hint of spiciness. If your palate is accustomed to foods with a bit of a kick, you can use the Thai chili pepper, which is very strong.

The chili pepper provides many opportunities to tailor dishes exactly the way you like them. One of its great features, after all, is its ability to enhance the flavor of other ingredients. Finding that perfect dose of spice not only flavors food, it can also awaken tones in the dish that are not particularly intense in themselves, but thanks to the pepper, become suddenly full of character and taste. This is the case with tofu, a soybean-based preparation whose elastic consistency and almost tasteless flavor is enriched by the ingredients it is cooked with; the Brazilian Besler's cherry chili pepper, for example, can turn a regular, humdrum tofu dish into an absolutely delicious and appetizing tour de force.

Peppers – the sweet, slightly spicy and aromatic Amazon from South America and tabasco – transform our take on meatballs and sauce, making an everyday dish something extraordinary, unusual, and deliciously memorable.

Among our starters you'll also find crispy and delicate Vietnamese spring-style rolls, with a dipping sauce that serves up all the strength of the Indonesian cabe besar.

We highlight the fresh, exotic taste of shrimp with lemongrass with the tiny salamandra pepper; don't let its size fool you, though. It packs a very spicy punch.

From Mexico, we get delicious vegetable fritters prepared with chickpea flour, beans and the medium spicy amiga peppers.

If you want to turn up the heat, add a pinch of red habanero to the sauce!

# SPICY OLIVES (OR *ALIVI CUNZATI*)

## INGREDIENTS FOR 4 PEOPLE

18 OZ (500 G) BRINED GREEN OLIVES
3 STALKS CELERY
5 CLOVES GARLIC
1 FRESH IDEALINO PEPPER
1 DRIED IDEALINO PEPPER
2 CARROTS

1 BUNCH PARSLEY
3 1/2 OUNCES (100 G) PREPARED PICKLED VEGETABLES
   (E.G. GIARDINIERA)
EXTRA VIRGIN OLIVE OIL (AS NEEDED)
SALT
1 3/4 OZ (50 ML) RED WINE VINEGAR

Drain the olives in brine, rinse under running water and drain well. Then pour into a measuring salad bowl.

Remove all of the hard parts from the parsley, leaving only the leaves. Wash and wipe dry with kitchen paper or a cloth. Drain the pickled vegetables, if you want to reduce their acidity, rinse under running water for a moment, then cut the vegetables into small pieces and combine them with the olives. Wash the carrots and peel them. Cut them into thin slices and then again in 2 parts. Wash the celery stalks, dry them and slice them thinly. Peel the garlic and chop finely. Wash and dry the peppers, use a pestle and mortar to crush the dried idealino and cut the fresh pepper into slices.

Coarsely chop half the parsley leaves and wrap in a damp cloth so that they remain fresh and beautiful. Pour all the vegetables into a bowl with the olives. Season with plenty of extra virgin olive oil, salt, vinegar and stir. Let stand for at least 1 day before serving so that the flavors can mix. When serving, decorate with fresh parsley and with slices of fresh idealino.

*Spicy olives (Alivi cunzati) are a seasoned dish of southern Italy and the Mediterranean basin. A favorite variety for this type of recipe is the fleshy pugliesi olives, which have a sweet flavor and crunchy texture. Always a hit at family get-togethers and parties, this simple dish can be an ideal appetizer or side dish. Tasty and delicious, spicy olives can be a great ingredient to enrich first and second courses. They taste best with a red wine, preferably from Southern Italy.*

# BOUZGENE BREAD
# WITH TOMATO SAUCE

## INGREDIENTS FOR 4 PEOPLE

*FOR THE BREAD:*
1 1/3 CUPS (250 G) DURUM FLOUR
4 TBSP (60 ML) OLIVE OIL
WATER (AS NEEDED)
1/2 TSP (3 G) SALT

*FOR THE SAUCE:*
2 RIPE TOMATOES
1 FRESH HARISSA CHILI PEPPER
EXTRA VIRGIN OLIVE OIL
SALT

Wash the tomatoes, then dry and cut them into small pieces, draining any excess water by leaving them in a colander for 5 minutes. Wash the harissa pepper, removing the stem and seeds and chop it finely (seeds are always very strong, removing them reduces the spiciness). Place the tomatoes and the pepper in a bowl, season with salt and 2 tablespoons of olive oil and keep in a cool place until they're needed.

Put the flour, salt, and 2 tablespoons of water in a bowl or on a wooden surface and knead. Using your hands, add warm water little by little as the flour absorbs it. Mash the mixture with your hands several times until the dough appears to be well mixed and smooth. To prevent the mixture from sticking to your hands, grease the dough with a little oil. When the dough is well worked, divide it into four balls; roll each ball on a floured board with a rolling pin (or the palm of the hand) until you have a disk roughly half a centimeter thick.

Grease a heavy, non-stick frying pan by wiping the surface with an oiled paper towel (be careful not to get it too oily). Heat the pan on high heat. Cook the bread until color and cracks begin to appear, flip and cook another 2 to 3 minutes. Cook all the slices one at a time and remember to always add another layer of oil on the surface of the pan, so that the bread does not stick and ruin. Serve with the tomato sauce.

*Bouzgene bread is a very high caloric food, prepared in a way that allows it to last for days at a time. Comparatively solid, it is perfect for sopping up sauces and condiments. The bread is of Algerian origins, with a flavor that perfectly accompanies a fresh and fragrant sauce. The sweetness of the bread mixes perfectly with the tangy tomato and spicy pepper. The ideal drink for this snack is very sweet mint tea.*

# TEMPURA AJI PEPPERS

*Difficulty of preparation: Medium-Difficult - Difficulty of cooking: Easy - Preparation time: 10 minutes - Cooking time: 5-7 minutes - Resting time: 1 hour*

## INGREDIENTS FOR 4 PEOPLE

8 AJI HABANERO CHILI PEPPERS

1 GLASS OF VERY COLD MINERAL WATER

1/2 CUP (60 G) OF FLOUR

2 TBSP + 2 TSP (20 G) OF POTATO STARCH

1 PINCH OF GINGER POWDER

VEGETABLE OIL

SALT

If you want a very light and crispy batter, equip yourself with a steel container and place in freezer for 1 hour before using it (the colder the temperature when you work the ingredients, the lighter the batter!) Then pour in: starch, 1 tablespoon of flour, a pinch of salt and a pinch of powdered ginger. Combine with cold water and stir with a whisk until the mixture is smooth and lump free. Let stand a few minutes in the freezer.

Meanwhile, wash the peppers (it's best to use latex gloves to avoid inflaming the skin) and dry them with a kitchen towel. Slit on one side so that they do not burst during cooking, and dip them in the flour in a way that the batter adheres better.

Heat the vegetable oil until it begins smoking, or until the thermometer reaches 180 degrees, dip the chilies into the batter (holding the petiole), slightly drain the excess and transfer them into the hot oil. Fry until the batter is white and crisp, then remove them, placing them on absorbent paper. Serve immediately (garnishing, if desired, with a few drops of soy sauce).

*"Aji amarillo" is the name by which this chili is named in Peru, its country of origin, it can be eaten fresh or in powder form and in this case is called "mirasol". It can be both mild and very spicy, but it is extremely tasty and fleshy. Given its personality, it is very suitable for seasoning raw fish (which is called ceviche in Peru) and soups. Pisco is the drink best enjoyed with this simple but effective recipe.*

# FRITTATA (OMELET) WITH HABANERO AND FRIARIELLI PEPPERS

Difficulty of preparation: Easy - Degree of difficulty: Medium-Easy - Preparation time: 10 minutes - Cooking time: 6 to 8 minutes

## INGREDIENTS FOR 4 PEOPLE

14 OZ (400 G) FRIARIELLI CHILI PEPPERS

4 EGGS

HABANERO CHILI POWDER (AS NEEDED)

1 FRESH IDEALINO CHILI PEPPER

1 CLOVE GARLIC

EXTRA VIRGIN OLIVE OIL

SALT

Wash the friarielli peppers and the fresh idealino, dry them gently and remove the stem, seeds and white parts, cutting them into thin slices and small pieces. Peel garlic, crush coarsely and brown in 1 tablespoon of oil over low heat, so that it does not burn. Remove the garlic when golden and add the chili, friarielli and salt (to your taste) and then stir to even out the flavors. Leave on high heat for about 5 minutes, then remove from heat and let cool.

In a bowl, beat the eggs with a pinch of salt and a pinch of habanero chili powder, add the peppers and stir. Heat a non-stick frying pain with 2 tablespoons of oil, letting the oil slide across the surface and edges, then pour on the mixture.

Cook the frittata over medium heat for about 3 to 4 minutes, checking the edges with a wooden spoon while the egg begins to coagulate, then with the help of a lid, flip the frittata and continue cooking for another 3 minutes. Remove from heat and, covered, let stand for about 2 minutes, then transfer the frittata to a serving dish.

*The habanero pepper is to be used with extreme care: it is very spicy and for those who are not used to that, it can be a very surprising experience. Measure it out according to your habits and tastes. The friarielli omelet is a very versatile dish: it can be served hot (this best brings out the aromatic characteristics of the pepper, cold, as a starter, a second along with a salad or on a picnic. In carrying out this recipe, make sure that the egg does not burn (medium heat, or a wide flame are recommended) A red wine, not too full-bodied, or a fresh rosé may accompany the omelet.*

# SPICY MEXICAN VEGETABLE FRITTERS

## INGREDIENTS FOR 4 PEOPLE

1 1/4 CUPS (150 G) CHICKPEA FLOUR

3 1/2 OZ (100 G) 00 FLOUR

7 OZ (200 G) MIXED BOILED BEANS

1 EGG

2 YELLOW ONIONS

1 CLOVE GARLIC

1 TSP (2 ML) BAKING SODA

1 TBSP (5 G) AMIGA CHILI POWDER

1 1/4 CUP (300 ML) PEANUT OIL

SALT

BLACK PEPPERCORNS

*FOR THE SAUCE:*

4 TBSP (65 G) PEELED, SLICED TOMATOES

4 CAPERS IN BRINE

SALT

1 PINCH OF RED HABANERO CHILI POWDER

Peel and finely chop the clove of garlic. Peel the onions and slice them thinly. Sift flour into a bowl, add baking soda, chili powder (to taste), a pinch of salt and freshly ground pepper. Beat the egg with a fork, add it to flour, mix the ingredients and cover with running water. Let the dough absorb enough water until you have a soft, smooth, dense and lump-free batter.

Drain the cooked beans. Rinse them under running water and then pour them into the batter along with the onions and garlic, stirring gently to mix the ingredients together. Heat a non-stick frying pan with peanut seed oil. When it's hot, pour the mixture in spoonfuls. Do not touch the fritters for at least 1 minute, until they harden and you can turn them over without damaging them. To flip the fritters without damaging them, use 2 spoons or a cake knife. Remove the fritters once they become golden brown and drain the excess oil on absorbent paper towels. Continue in this way until you've finished all the dough.

When preparing the tomato sauce, season with salt, chili powder and sliced capers, mix and put into a bowl. Just before serving, make cones out of paper, fill them with fritters and place it on the dish. Serve with the tomato sauce.

*Vegetable fritters are a very informal, tasty and appetizing "guilty pleasure", in the truest sense of the term. Nutritious and delicious, fritters are perfectly original and fun appetizer. The perfect wine can be a full-bodied red like a Tuscan, but also a playful and well-chilled white.*

# TOFU CUBES WITH SICHUAN PEPPER

## INGREDIENTS FOR 4 PEOPLE

1 LB (500 G) TOFU

2 TBSP (30 ML) SOY SAUCE

1 TSP (2 G) CHOPPED BESLER'S CHERRY CHILI
PEPPER

6 2/3 OZ (200 ML) CHICKEN BROTH

2 TSP (5 G) CORNSTARCH

2 CLOVES GARLIC

1 TSP (2 G) GROUND SICHUAN PEPPER

1 TBSP (15 ML) PEANUT OIL

Rinse and dry the tofu, then cut into cubes of 3 to 4 inches. Heat the broth and keep hot until ready to use. Pour the oil in a wok and place it on the stove over medium heat. When the oil is hot, add the soy sauce and half the pepper, stirring and cooking for about 1 minute. Then add the broth and the tofu, reducing the heat and letting it simmer gently for about 4 minutes, stirring regularly, but very gently so that the tofu does not break.

Meanwhile, dissolve the cornstarch in a tablespoon of cold water and stir until smooth, with no lumps. Add it to the tofu in the wok. Peel the garlic, chop finely and add it to the other ingredients, cooking for another 1 minute, then remove from heat.

When serving, separate from the tofu sauce, let it drain on a wooden cutting board, gently dabbing with paper towels. Arrange in a serving dish and then sprinkle with Sichuan pepper. Decorate with peppers and serve.

*This recipe originated in China and can be a tasty base with which to accompany other ingredients, such as shrimp or vegetables. Tofu is made from soybeans, and is also called "bean curd". It is rich in protein and suitable for complete vegetarian and vegan diets. It has a neutral flavor, soft but compact texture and takes the flavor and taste of the seasonings and food with which it is prepared. The ideal drink to taste this dish is definitely green tea.*

# MEATBALLS WITH LIME SAUCE

## INGREDIENTS FOR 4 PEOPLE

14 OZ (400 G) CHICKEN BREAST

3 AMAZON CHILI PEPPERS

3 EGGS

2 TBSP (15 G) FLOUR

1 3/4 OZ (50 G) GRATED CHEESE

7 OZ (200 G) BREAD CRUMBS

1 1/4 CUP (300 ML) VEGETABLE OIL

3 1/2 OZ (100 G) GREENS OR SPINACH

SALT

FOR THE SAUCE:

1 RIPE AVOCADO

1 SMALL ONION

1 PINCH TABASCO CHILI POWDER

HALF A LIME

SALT

Chop the peppers. Grate the cheese. Cut the chicken into pieces, then cook at high heat, adding salt to taste. Stir and remove from heat. Chop finely or use a mixer and pour into a container. Add 2 eggs, cheese, peppers and stir until everything is well blended and firm. Pour into a bowl and whisk the egg with a fork. Pour the white flour and bread crumb into 2 different containers. With your hands, form balls the size of a quail egg and coat them first in flour, then egg and finally in the breadcrumbs so that it all adheres well.

Before cooking the meatballs, prepare the sauce. Peel the onion and chop finely. Peel the avocado, removing the seeds and any dark portions, then flatten with the prongs of a fork. Add salt and chili powder to taste, the juice of half a lime, onion and stir until you have smooth sauce and let stand until use.

Pour the oil in a non-stick frying pan, and once the heat reaches 180 degrees, dip in the meatballs. When they start to brown, flip them to ensure homogeneous baking. After about 3 to 4 minutes of total cooking, drain and dry the excess oil on absorbent paper. Just before serving the dish, lay out the dish with herbs, the meatballs and a bowl of the lime sauce.

*Frying is one of the most delicious and tasty cooking methods the world of cuisine has to offer. Croquettes and fried meatballs in particular are the result of imagination and ingenuity: there can always be surprises in the breading, meat, vegetables and cheeses used, creating a triumph of taste with a simple dip in hot oil. Excellent as an aperitif or appetizer (provided they are hot and steaming), this dish is perfect with a nice mug of beer.*

# CEVICHE WITH TOMATO AND PEPPER

## INGREDIENTS FOR 4 PEOPLE

14 OZ (400 G) SWORDFISH CARPACCIO

3 LEMONS

2 RIPE BUT FIRM TOMATOES

1 RED BELL PEPPER

1 FRESH CONQUISTADOR CHILI PEPPER

8 TSP (10 G) OF CHOPPED CILANTRO

SALT

Spread the slices of fish in a container with edges. Squeeze the juice from 2 lemons and let the fish slices "cook" for about 10 minutes. Meanwhile, wash the tomatoes, cut in cubes, remove the seeds and let the excess water drain in a colander. Wash the peppers, removing the stem, seeds and white parts. Cut about 8 to 10 long, thin strips for decoration and the remainder into small pieces.

Remove all the hard parts from the cilantro, keeping just the leaves. Wash, dry gently with paper towels and chop. Drain the fish (now "whitewashed" from the marinade) and arrange the slices on individual plates, placing the vegetables and decorating with strips of bell pepper. Halve the lemon and then cut slices to decorate the plate.

Wash the chili peppers, removing the seeds, stem and white parts (be careful, remember to use latex gloves to avoid irritating the skin). Distribute it on the ceviche, add salt to taste, cilantro for flavor and squeeze a few drops of lemon juice. Serve at room temperature or after a sitting in the fridge for 10 minutes.

*Marinated raw fish is a delicacy that is simple to prepare but very effective. You can use different types of fish, giving priority to larger breeds with fewer bones, and firm and compact flesh. Lightweight and easy to digest, this dish is perfect for the summer and very popular in warmer countries that border the sea. In the Mediterranean, the recipe always has a few drops of extra virgin olive oil, while in South America, the marinade also involves lime. You can accompany this appetizer with chilled dry white wine or a pisco savor.*

# GARLIC, PARSLEY AND PEPPER MUSSELS

## INGREDIENTS FOR 4 PEOPLE

3 1/3 LB (1.5 KG) FRESH MUSSELS

1/8 TSP (1 G) DRIED IDEALINO CHILI PEPPER

1 FRESH CABE BESAR CHILI PEPPER

2 CLOVES GARLIC

2/3 CUP (40 G) PARSLEY

1/4 CUP (50 ML) EXTRA VIRGIN OLIVE OIL

1 TBSP (12 G) COARSE SALT

Carefully clean the mussels with a knife, removing the beard (the filaments protruding from the shells) and scrub them thoroughly. Wash again in running water and then leave them to soak in 1 tablespoon of coarse salt for about 1 hour. From time to time, move them around in the water. Once they've soaked, put them back under plenty of running water and then drain them.

Clean the parsley, wash it and gently dry it with paper towels, then chop. Peel the garlic and mash with a fork. Finally, cut the fresh pepper in slices.

Pour the oil in a skillet large enough to allow the mussels to open. On medium heat, sauté the garlic, combine with half the chopped fresh chili pepper, add the mussels and turn the heat up. Cover and let the mussels open, stirring regularly so that everything is cooked evenly. Add the parsley, the remaining part of the fresh cabe besar pepper rings and the dried chili pepper and remove from heat. Stir and serve immediately.

*This is a light, tasty, and very easy to prepare dish, ideal as a starter and as a undemanding main course. Very popular in almost all Mediterranean countries, it is most often prepared in traditional manners (respective to each country or region). Preparation time can be significantly reduced by buying mussels that are ready to be cooked. You can accompany this dish with a chilled white wine (such as a Vermentino or Pigato) that emphasizes the intense flavor without overwhelming the dish.*

# KING PRAWNS SAUTÉED
# WITH CHILI AND LEMONGRASS

## INGREDIENTS FOR 4 PEOPLE

20 PRAWN TAILS

1 STALK OF LEMONGRASS

4 SALAMANDRA CHILI PEPPERS

1 BUNCH OF PARSLEY

2 TBSP (30 ML) OLIVE OIL

1 CLOVE OF GARLIC

SALT

Peel the lemongrass, removing the final part of the leaves, the tough and leathery outer leaves and cut into slices. Clean the parsley, wash and wipe dry with paper towels, then chop finely. Wash the peppers and cut into 2 parts lengthwise.

Remove the shell from the prawns, leaving the end part for a greater visual effect. With a paring knife, cut a slit on the dorsal side, right where you see a dark bead. Very gently (it breaks easily) remove this bead: it is the bowel, and sometimes, it contains grains of sand. Gently wash and pat dry with paper towels.

Pour the oil in a pan, let it heat. Mash the garlic and let brown, when fragrant, add the pepper, the lemongrass and shrimp. Stir and cook over high heat for about 1 minute or until you see that the transparent flesh of the shellfish has become white. Just before removing from the heat, salt and add parsley. Serve hot.

*The prawns need to be cooked fast: cooking them can take seconds (maximum 1 minute).*
*In fact, if you exceed this ideal cooking time, their delicate flesh becomes tough and rubbery.*
*Keep a close eye on the color when cooking, as when the meat loses its transparency, is time*
*to remove them from the heat! Perfect for a delicious appetizer, shrimp can even be enjoyed*
*by those who do not usually have a taste for flavors of the sea. In this case the chili pepper*
*enriches the gentle personality of the shrimp and the lemongrass provides an exotic, fresh taste.*
*A glass of sparkling wine is the perfect drink for this dish.*

# VIETNAMESE ROLLS
# WITH SPICY SAUCE

Difficulty of preparation: Medium - Difficulty of cooking: Easy - Preparation time: 30 minutes - Cooking time: 3-4 minutes

## INGREDIENTS FOR 4 PEOPLE

16 ROUND RICE PAPER SHEETS

3 1/2 OZ (100 G) CRABMEAT

1 TBSP (14 G) CHOPPED SHRIMP

3 1/2 OZ (100 G) LEAN MINCED PORK

1 3/4 OZ (50 G) SOY NOODLES

5 SPRING ONIONS

2 TBSP (2 G) CHOPPED FRESH CILANTRO

1 1/4 CUPS (300 ML) SUNFLOWER OIL

SALT AND PEPPER

3 1/3 OZ (100 G) SALAD

2 CARROTS CUT INTO MATCHSTICKS

*FOR THE SAUCE:*

1 CHOPPED CABE BESAR CHILI PEPPER

2 CLOVES OF GARLIC (CHOPPED)

1 TBSP (9 G) BROWN SUGAR

1 LIME

1 TBSP (15 ML) RICE VINEGAR

4 TBSP (60 ML) FISH BROTH

Peel the onions and finely chop both the white and green parts. Soak the noodles in boiling water for 10 minutes, then drain and remove any irregular pieces. Pour into a bowl, add the ground beef, fresh cilantro, spring onions, crab meat and chopped shrimp. Stir, adding salt and pepper to taste. Soak the rice sheets in cold water, one at a time, then put them on a linen or cotton cloth. Fill them with a tablespoon of filling and seal by folding the sides first and then wrapping to form a cylinder. In order to seal them well, wet the ends so that the dough sticks well. Proceed in this way until you have finished up the ingredients.

Before cooking, prepare the sauce by combining the following in a bowl: chilies, garlic, sugar, freshly squeezed lime juice, vinegar and fish stock. Stir well until you have a unified compound. Leave in the fridge until use.

Pour 3 ounces of oil into a wok or a pan. When hot (about 180 degrees), dip the rolls, making sure they are floating. When crisp and golden brown (it only takes about 3 to 4 minutes on high heat) remove with a slotted spoon. Transfer them to paper towels to remove any excess oil. Just before serving, arrange lettuce and carrots in the dish and place the rolls on top of this bed. Serve with the sauce.

*Rolls like these are now known all over the world thanks to their delicious taste, and the spread of Asian restaurants. There are many versions: vegetables, pork, fish, but they all seem to feature aromatic herbs, fragrant spicy sauces and seasonings. They are usually offered with sweet and sour or spicy sauces. Black tea is the best drink to accompany Vietnamese rolls, however, a good, dry (and chilled) white wine can also work wonders.*

# RED PEPPERS STUFFED WITH TUNA, ANCHOVIES AND CAPERS

*Difficulty of preparation: Easy - Difficulty of cooking: Easy - Preparation time: 2 hours - Cooking time: 3 minutes - Resting time: 12 hours*

## MAKES 4 CUPS / 1000 G

2.2 LB (1 KG) BRITISH, DELICATE OR THAI CHILI PEPPERS

14 OZ (400 G) TUNA IN OIL, DRAINED

7 OZ (200 G) ANCHOVIES IN OIL

5 1/4 OZ (150 G) PICKLED CAPERS

2 1/8 CUPS (500 ML) EXTRA VIRGIN OLIVE OIL

2 1/8 CUPS (500 ML) WHITE VINEGAR

SALT

Wash the peppers, with a knife cut off the stem and remove the seeds inside with a spoon. For this, it's best to use gloves to protect your skin from the capsaicin found in the chili pepper, which can be irritating to the skin. Work the peppers gently so that they do not break and can accommodate a filling. Finish cleaning them, and let them rest in a colander. Boil the vinegar with water and the equivalent of half a teaspoon of salt. When boiling, dip in the peppers and after 2 - 3 minutes, drain and put them upside down on kitchen towels. Let dry for about 12 hours, turning occasionally and replacing the towels.

Chop the tuna on a plate with the prongs of a fork, then stuff half the peppers with the tuna, the other half with the capers and anchovy fillets. As they are stuffed, arrange them in glass jars (to better show off what's inside!), making sure that the stuffing does not come out, and leaving as little space as possible between them. To complete the preserve, add oil up to the brim and close the jars.

To preserve the stuffed peppers for a few months, sterilize the jars, boiling them while wrapped in kitchen towels for 20 minutes. Then let it cool in the water. Remove them and store in a cool, dark, dry place.

*This wonderful appetizer has a starring role on tables all over Italy. Once upon a time, this preserve was prepared in late summer and stored for the winter (when fresh vegetables were a distant memory), bringing the color and flavor of warmer months to the coldest season of the year. With its bright colors and mix of flavors, stuffed peppers are a balanced and delicious dish that can be used as a side for many fish-based main courses. An excellent, fresh white wine (like Grillo di Sicilia) would work best as an accompaniment.*

# FIRST COURSES

The first course dishes cannot start with anything other than a pasta, that exquisite preparation common to many countries, but which, in Italy, is the queen of the table: the most appetizing dishes probably come right from the Italian peninsula. Besides those that have already affirmed themselves, new specialties are always being added. Italy also has a great love for the chili pepper, the spicy and delicious note present in many traditional recipes. Lately, due to the ever more pressing pace of life, the first course dish has become a single course meal, and thus the pasta dish has been enriched with various ingredients and with fish, meat, and vegetables. Purists of this foodstuff also associate the shapes that are ideal for one type or another of sauce or condiment. Also belonging to the vast family of pasta, the delicious Sardinian fregola is a dried pasta made from durum wheat semolina and worked by hand. It is quite similar to couscous, although less well known. Result: a lot of taste and goodness, for a very satisfying meal! First course dishes form an ideal match with the chili pepper. This is a given fact: the sweetness of the pasta blends so well with the spiciness of capsicum that it transforms any shape of pasta, from spaghetti to trofie, into an unforgettable delicacy. But which chili pepper is best to use for pasta? Is it better to use fresh, minced, powdered, or in paste form? Dried chili peppers are always excellent and they are easy to conserve: they are collected in braids or placed in pots and then crumbled at the instant they are needed. They adorn the preparation, in addition to flavoring, and they are ideal for seasoning sauces, whether rich or of few ingredients. It is advisable to use the powdered form when it needs to blend completely into a creamy, enveloping sauce, while fresh chili peppers are perfect for salads or dishes where an ingredient's fragrant notes and richness in water are to be perceived. It is a short step from pasta dishes to rice dishes. And for this delicious staple foodstuff as well, this matching of sweet and spicy is natural for a good part of the world: it is almost spontaneous to enrich the white grains with the exuberance of chili peppers. Just as for pasta, it often happens that a rice dish takes the place of a full meal, and so a bit of fantasy creates special dishes that are different every day: just one ingredient, such as salmon, beans, or oranges, and then just a pinch of habanero or jalapeño pepper unleashes a particular fire, filled with flavor. The chili pepper is also energy, heat, concentrated in the red of the fruit; its energy does not stop at the plate, and the exuberance of the food becomes a burst of spirit entering into us! It may seem excessive to speak about chili pepper in this way, but it is true that it is not simply a food: it is an experience, and there are so many different flavors and degrees of strength that it can truly be said to be within range of everyone's taste. And there's nothing better than a first course dish based on carbohydrates (which are suites to the palate) for a dive into the world of spiciness. We can range from cayenne peppers to tabasco; from the jalapeño to the habanero for a stronger, almost uncontrollable, impact; or we can allow ourselves to be enveloped by the exotic caresses of the suavito, the cheiro, the chili de onza, or the belviola, without any particular expectations of taste other than an encounter with food that can give so much. And our journey through first course dishes concludes with soups, in the enveloping consistencies based on coconut and on the spicy anda, amid delicious mollusks and small pieces of tabasco, amid a bouillabaisse with its significant flavor accompanied by the gentle delicate, or in the Thai chicken with the indiano, and in the velvet creaminess of the squash, enveloped in the flavor of the british.

# SPAGHETTI AGLIO OLIO E PEPERONCINO

Difficulty of preparation: Easy - Degree of difficulty: Easy - Preparation time: 5 minutes - Cooking time: 8-10 minutes

## INGREDIENTS FOR 4 PEOPLE
3/4 LB (350 G) SPAGHETTI
4 CLOVES GARLIC
2 ABBRACCIO RED CHILI PEPPERS
3 1/2 TBSP (50 ML) EXTRA VIRGIN OLIVE OIL
SALT

Set 4 cups (1 L) of salted water to boil in a pot. Peel the garlic and cut into slices. Wash the chili peppers, remove the stems, and slice.

Pour the oil into a nonstick pan and heat; when quite hot, add the chili pepper and garlic. This is a very simple seasoning, but in order to make it perfect, the garlic should turn golden, without burning or drying out, therefore check the flame very carefully so that the garlic turns out "soft" cooked. After 2 minutes of continually mixing the ingredients with a wooden spoon, remove from the heat and let stand until ready to use.

When the water boils, add the spaghetti and cook for the amount of time indicated on the package. When cooked al dente, drain the spaghetti well and add to the pan with the seasoning. Mix well and serve quite hot.

*Pasta Aglio Olio e Peperoncino – a very simple recipe but very effective and remarkably tasty – holds the record for the quickest first course dish! Just a few minutes and voilà, the dish is ready! It is also said that the chili pepper has aphrodisiac powers. We cannot say for sure, but there is no doubt that the richness on the palate of pasta with garlic, oil, and chili pepper makes this dish particularly satisfying. A decisive and robust red wine is the ideal accompaniment for completing a meal centered on this dish.*

# CONCHIGLIE WITH FRAGRANCES OF PANTELLERIA

## INGREDIENTS FOR 4 PEOPLE

3/4 LB (350 G) CONCHIGLIE TYPE PASTA

3/4 OZ (20 G) PANTELLERIA CAPERS, SALTED

4 TOMATOES, RIPE AND FIRM

1 CLOVE GARLIC

1 SPRIG DRIED OREGANO

1 ACRATA RED CHILI PEPPER

EXTRA VIRGIN OLIVE OIL

SALT

Set the capers in water to eliminate the excess salt, then wash repeatedly in running water. Drain well then coarsely chop half the capers. Peel and chop the garlic. Eliminate the hard portions of the oregano and chop finely. Peel the tomatoes, immersing first in boiling water for 30 seconds, then remove the peels, cut into wedges, remove the seeds and hard parts, chop into pieces, and drain off the excess water in a sieve.

Wash the chili pepper, remove the stem and seeds, then slice into rounds. Heat 4 tablespoons of olive oil in a nonstick pan. When hot, sauté the garlic with half the oregano, the coarsely chopped capers, the whole capers, and the chili pepper. Mix well to blend the various flavors. Add the tomato and let reduce by half. During the cooking (over medium heat this may be about 10 minutes), salt to taste.

Cook the pasta in plenty of salted boiling water for the amount of time indicated on the package. When cooked al dente, drain and pour into the pan with the seasoning. Mix well and, if desired, add another couple of tablespoons of olive oil. Serve the conchiglie in individual plates, sprinkle with the remaining oregano, and serve immediately.

*In Pantelleria, the fragrances are remarkably decisive and well defined, perhaps because of the wind that constantly caresses the island, giving an air so clean you can distinctly perceive all the tones of the Mediterranean maquis. Even the oregano growing spontaneously among the dry-mounted stone walls has an entirely original fragrance, wild and decisive. This simple and easy to make pasta dish embodies all the personality of the island, now a part of Sicily but still conserving traces of the Arab domination, a heritage that emerges in the decisive and languid flavors of this hot and strong territory. For a wine, aromatic full-bodied white Zibibbo makes the perfect complement for a pasta dish so heartily flavored of sun and wind.*

# SPICY ORECCHIETTE WITH BROCCOLI

*Difficulty of preparation: Medium-Difficult - Degree of difficulty: Easy - Preparation time: 60-90 minutes - Cooking time: 15-20 minutes*

## INGREDIENTS FOR 4 PEOPLE

*FOR THE ORECCHIETTE:*
2/3 LB (300 G) DURUM WHEAT FLOUR ("RIMACINATA,"
   THE TYPE SUITABLE FOR MAKING "ALTAMURA" OR
   "PUGLIESE" TYPE BREAD)
WATER, AS NEEDED
OIL
SALT

*FOR THE SEASONING:*
1 LB (500 G) BROCCOLI
2 CLOVES GARLIC
1 FRESH IDEALINO RED CHIILI PEPPER
6 TBSP (90 ML) EXTRA VIRGIN OLIVE OIL
SALT
1 3/4 OZ (50 G) AGED PECORINO CHEESE,
   GRATED (OPTIONAL)

Arrange the flour on the work surface, making a well in the center. Pour half a cup of tepid water and a pinch of salt into the well. Work together the ingredients until obtaining a smooth, firm, and elastic mixture. At this point, work the dough, taking a portion at a time, and covering the rest of the dough with a moist cloth so it does not dry. Form a portion of dough into a salami shape with a diameter of about 3/4 inch (2 cm). Using a knife, cut little rounds about half a centimeter in thickness, and squash them against a floured surface using your thumb so they take on the classic "shell" form. On a floured cloth, let dry the orecchiette you have thus formed, separated well from one another. Continue the process until all the dough has been formed into orecchiette.

Trim the broccoli, wash, and separate into florets. Set plenty of salted water in a pot to boil, and when boiling, pour in the orecchiette. During this time, peel the garlic, cut into slices, and sauté until golden in a pan with 2 tablespoons of the oil. Add the broccoli, then season with the chili pepper cut into small pieces. Salt and let everything cook over a lively flame for 5 minutes, stirring from time to time.

A few minutes before draining the orecchiette, increase the heat under the pan with the seasoning, allowing any remaining moisture to evaporate. Drain the pasta and add to the sauce, mix well, and serve at the table. Serve with a dish of grated aged Pecorino cheese as accompaniment.

*This recipe recounts the tradition of Pugliese cuisine, the manifesto of the Mediterranean cuisine, where vegetables and grain are the base of the daily diet: flavors that are simple but decisive, a perfect balance between freshness and fragrance. This dish can be served in the warm months as well as the cold, because it is well equilibrated in nutrients and is not heavy to digest. Best served with a fresh and light dry white wine.*

# PASTA WITH MEDITERRANEAN FLAVORS

## INGREDIENTS FOR 4 PEOPLE

3/4 LB (350 G) SPAGHETTI

1 OZ (30 G) ANCHOVY FILLETS IN OIL

3 1/2 OZ (100 G) TOMATO PURÉE

3 1/2 OZ (100 G) BLACK OLIVES, PITTED

3/4 OZ (20 G) PANTELLERIA CAPERS, SALTED

1/3 OZ (10 G) PARSLEY

1 SALAMANDRA CHILI PEPPER

1 CLOVE GARLIC

EXTRA VIRGIN OLIVE OIL

SALT

Drain the olives and cut into small pieces. Soak the capers in cold water for 5 minutes, then wash repeatedly under running water to eliminate the excess salt. Trim and clean the parsley; chop finely. Chop the chili pepper. Peel the garlic and crush coarsely using the blade of a knife.

Pour 2 tablespoons of olive oil into a nonstick pan sufficiently large to contain both the sauce and pasta. Heat over high flame and add the chili pepper and garlic, which you can eliminate after it has turned golden. Add the anchovies and let dissolve over low heat, mixing them into the oil. Now add the tomato purée, lower the flame, and let simmer for about 20 minutes, stirring from time to time. Taste and if necessary correct for salt (keeping in mind that the capers, even after washing, contain quite a bit of salt).

In a pot, bring to a boil plenty of salted water and cook the spaghetti for a minute less than the time indicated on the package. Drain and pour into the sauce. Heat the pasta and sauce mixture and stir. Add the capers, olives, parsley, and 2 more tablespoons of olive oil, as needed. Serve immediately.

*Pantelleria capers are a delicacy containing all the magic of the flavors of that island, where the elements show no half measures. The flavor that develops from these small buds is unforgettable, becoming one of the most sought-after ingredients for preparing a pasta dish with an authentically Mediterranean personality. In this dish, the chili pepper is not only a normal ingredient, but the key element that binds and emphasizes the all-Sicilian flavor of the recipe. Best served with a Chardonnay from the island, young and well chilled, for a complete immersion into the flavors of Sicily.*

# BUCATINI ALL'AMATRICIANA

## INGREDIENTS FOR 4 PEOPLE

3/4 LB (350 G) BUCATINI-TYPE PASTA

1/3 LB (150 G) CURED PORK JOWL OR PANCETTA
   (BACON)

1 ONION

1 IDEALINO OR BODY GUARD CHILI PEPPER

5 TO 6 PERINO (SAN MARZANO) TOMATOES, QUITE RIPE

3 1/2 OZ (100 G) PECORINO ROMANO CHEESE

2 TBSP (30 ML) EXTRA VIRGIN OLIVE OIL

SALT

Dunk the tomatoes into boiling water, so that the skin separates more easily from the pulp. Remove them from the water using a slotted spoon or skimmer, peel, and remove the seeds and any hard parts. Cut the pork jowl into small chunks, then sauté in the oil and drain when crunchy and reduced by half (after about 2-3 minutes).

Peel the onion and slice finely, then sauté along with the pork jowl mixture. Keep the flame law so that the onion turns golden but remains soft. While cooking, add the chili pepper, washed and finely chopped. When the onion has turned soft, add the tomato fillets and let cook for 10 minutes, stirring often.

Bring to a boil plenty of salted water and cook the bucatini pasta. When immersing the pasta into the water, use a wooden spoon to ease the bucatini in, taking care not to let them break. Let cook for the time indicated on the package, then drain and transfer into the pan with the sauce. During the cooking time, grate the the cheese and distribute over the seasoned pasta. Serve quite hot, so that the intense aromas of the pork jowl and Pecorino cheese can be best appreciated.

*The dish of pasta made "Amatriciana" style is an invention from the small village of Amatrice, in the province of Rieti. Initially, the recipe did not call for tomato, which was added later, with the "Romanization" of the dish, which originally reflected the Abruzzi influence more than that from Lazio. The recipe is very easy, but very good: the different ingredients meld perfectly with one another, releasing fragrances and flavors unexpected for a dish so simple to make. The chili pepper binds together the few but important ingredients, for outstanding flavor. Best enjoyed with an intense and full-bodied red wine, for flavors with such intense personalities as the pork jowl and Pecorino cheese.*

# PENNE ALL'ARRABBIATA

## INGREDIENTS FOR 4 PEOPLE

3/4 LB (350 G) PENNE RIGATE TYPE PASTA

3 1/2 OZ (100 G) PECORINO ROMANO CHEESE

2 IDEALINO CHILI PEPPERS

4 TOMATOES, RIPE AND FIRM

3/4 OZ (20 G) PARSLEY

2 CLOVES GARLIC

EXTRA VIRGIN OLIVE OIL

SALT

Trim the parsley, then wash and dry by gently patting with paper towel. Finely chop the parsley. Peel and chop the garlic.

Dunk the tomatoes into boiling water. After 30 seconds, remove it using a slotted spoon or skimmer. Peel the tomatoes, removing the seeds and any hard parts. Chop into small cubes and let the pulp drain in a sieve. Wash the chili peppers, remove the stems and seeds, and slice into rounds. (The seeds of the Solanaceae family are generally the hottest part, so with this in mind, keep or remove them depending on your approach to spiciness.) Grate the Pecorino cheese and set aside until time for use.

Into a nonstick pan sufficiently large for sautéing both the sauce and the pasta after cooking, pour 4 tablespoons of olive oil, and sauté the garlic and chili pepper. Add the tomatoes, salt to taste, and let the sauce reduce by half (about 8-10 minutes over medium-lively flame). Bring to a boil 1 L (or 1 quart) of salted water, pour in the penne and let cook according to the instructions on the package. When cooked, drain and transfer into the pan with the sauce. Sauté altogether over lively flame for 30 seconds, allowing the flavors to blend well, then remove from the heat. Sprinkle with the cheese and parsley, mix, and serve immediately.

*Penne all'Arrabbiata is one of the traditional culinary dishes from Lazio, one that over time has infected and seduced nearly the entire Italian peninsula. The recipe is very simple and easy to prepare, requiring however a few key observations to make sure it comes out perfect: the garlic should be sautéed delicately over a gentle flame so that it does not become woody and bitter; the chili pepper dose should be calibrated to perfectly match the sharpness of the cheese; and the pasta should have the crunchy texture characteristic of Italian durum wheat. A goblet of dry white wine accompanies this first course dish outstandingly.*

# THE FISHERMAN'S CLASSIC: SPICY SPAGHETTI WITH BOTTARGA

## INGREDIENTS FOR 4 PEOPLE

3/4 LB (350 G) SPAGHETTI (MEDIUM)
14 OZ (400 G) CHERRY TOMATOES
1 1/2 OZ (40 G) MULLET BOTTARGA
2 DRIED IDEALINO CHILI PEPPERS

1/3 OZ (10 G) PARSLEY
EXTRA VIRGIN OLIVE OIL
SALT

Wash the cherry tomatoes, dry, and cut into four wedges each. Place into a bowl, and add in the equivalent of 4 tablespoons of olive oil. Trim and wash the parsley, gently pat dry with a kitchen cloth, and finely chop.

Wash the chili pepper, dry, and grind in a mortar. In a pot bring to a boil plenty of salted water and cook the pasta for the time indicated on the package. Meanwhile, grate the bottarga.

Drain the pasta, pour into the bowl with the cherry tomatoes, add the bottarga, the parsley, and the chili pepper. Mix well, then distribute into the individual plates; serve immediately.

*Here is a very tasty dish that can be prepared in record time, but without compromising on flavor, which is truly excellent. Be careful not to add too much salt, because the bottarga, which is made from the roe of the silver mullet, is conserved using abundant salt, becoming a delicious food element that transforms a simple plate into a delicacy. This pasta is a first course dish that is sure to please: bottarga balances perfectly with the spiciness of the chili pepper, to be dosed to your liking to obtain the proper balance. This recipe, Italian in origin, comes from traditional peasant cooking, from the villages on the sea toward the south. It is said that at one time, fishermen were paid in sacks of fish roe, and that they dried them to conserve them. Since it is a highly nutritious foodstuff, just a small amount on bread or pasta sufficed for facing a day of work. A white wine from Sicily or Calabria – fresh, fragrant, fruity – makes the ideal accompaniment for this dish.*

# THE CLASSIC SPAGHETTI ALLE VONGOLE

Difficulty of preparation: Easy - Degree of difficulty: Easy - Preparation time: 1 hour - Cooking time: 10-12 minutes

## INGREDIENTS FOR 4 PEOPLE

3/4 LB (350 G) SPAGHETTI

1 3/4 LB (800 G) CLAMS

2 CLOVES GARLIC

2 TABASCO CHILI PEPPERS

3/4 OZ (20 G) PARSLEY

4 TBSP EXTRA VIRGIN OLIVE OIL

COARSE SALT

Make sure all your clams are closed, and eliminate any that are not. Wash under running water, and let soak in plenty of water salted with two large spoons of coarse salt. Trim the parsley, removing the hard parts, keeping only the leaves; wash, pat dry with paper towel, and finely chop. Peel the garlic and finely chop. Wash the chili pepper and chop into small pieces.

Drain the clams, rinse once more under running water, and let drain in a colander. Let them open in a pan with dry heat (that is, with no condiments), then remove from the heat. This process will allow you to check once again, so you can remove any shells that may still be filled with sand. Remove the mollusks from the half the shells, leaving the rest intact. Filter the water that has been released, and keep aside until time for use.

Set plenty of salted water to boil in a large pot. Peel the garlic, and sauté in olive oil in a pan with a thick bottom, large enough to contain the pasta and sauce together. While sautéing, add the chili peppers and the mollusks. Mix everything well and let cook over high heat for a few minutes. Season with the parsley, mix, and remove from the heat. Boil the pasta for one minute less than the time indicated on the package. Drain and pour into the pan with the sauce. Sauté over high heat, mixing well to blend the flavors. Add a few tablespoons of the clam broth and serve immediately.

*Pasta – in all its forms – is one of the favorite Italian dishes, famous throughout the world. Spaghetti alle Vongole is a classic. Its flavor is simple, but at the same time complex, with the fresh scent of the sea, the perfect spiciness of the chili pepper, and the fragrance of the parsley creating a rare harmony of flavors that is loved all throughout the peninsula. The best periods to appreciate this dish are certainly late spring and summer. A fresh aromatic white wine is the beverage that perfectly complements this dish, one of the top in Italian cuisine.*

# "ANDEAN" LINGUINE
# WITH CRUSTACEANS AND SEAFOOD

## INGREDIENTS FOR 4 PEOPLE

3/4 LB (350 G) LINGUINE-TYPE PASTA

8 LANGOUSTINES

8 SHRIMP

1 LB (500 G) CLAMS

2.2 LB (1 KG) MUSSELS

0.66 LB (300 G) TUFTS OF SMALL SQUID

5 SMALL ANDA CHILI PEPPERS

3/4 OZ (20 G) PARSLEY

2 CLOVES GARLIC

EXTRA VIRGIN OLIVE OIL

COARSE SALT

Clean the mussels, removing the byssus (the beard-like part that comes out of the mussels), and scraping the shells using a wire brush. Set to soak in water with a large spoon of coarse salt and let rest for 30 minutes. Proceed in the same manner with the clams, keeping separate from the mussels. Wash the scampi, the shrimps, and the squid tufts (if large, cut into pieces, otherwise leave whole).

Remove the tough parts from the parsley, wash, pat dry, and finely chop. Wash one of the chili peppers and slice into rounds. Drain the mussels and clams. Open the clams in a pan using dry heat (without adding any condiments) and after a few minutes, remove from the fire, checking to be sure that none of the shells are filled with sand. Remove the mollusks from half the shells and keep aside in a bowl until time for use. Pour 2 tablespoons of oil into a nonstick pan, sauté the garlic, unpeeled, and the chili pepper, then add the mussels and let open over maximum heat. If the mussels release very much liquid, eliminate half the liquid. Now add the squid tufts, the scampi, shrimps, and clams. Mix and remove from the heat.

Set the linguine to boil in a pot of plenty of salted water, and drain one minute earlier than the time indicated on the package. Pour into the pan with the sauce and sauté over high heat. Serve in dishes and sprinkle with the parsley and the chili peppers, cut lengthwise.

*Not only very attractive, this dish is a great success, just right for an informal lunch: to best enjoy the richness of this pasta dish, in fact, it is preferable to use your hands as well, covering yourself, of course, first with a napkin! This spicy version of Linguine allo Scoglio is a magnificent preparation, best enjoyed with a glass of chilled bubbly white wine.*

# LINGUINE WITH AMBERJACK

Difficulty of preparation: Easy - Degree of difficulty: Easy - Preparation time: 15 minutes - Cooking time: 10-12 minutes

## INGREDIENTS FOR 4 PEOPLE

3/4 LB (350 G) LINGUINE-TYPE PASTA

14 OZ (400 G) TOMATOES, RIPE BUT FIRM

2/3 LB (300 G) AMBERJACK (YELLOWTAIL)

3/4 OZ + 1 TBSP (25 G) PARSLEY

2 CLOVES GARLIC

1 DRIED IDEALINO CHILI PEPPER

EXTRA VIRGIN OLIVE OIL

SALT

Remove all the tough parts from the parsley, wash the leaves, gently pat dry with paper towel, and chop three or four sprigs. Peel the garlic, and crumble the chili pepper in a mortar. Wash the fish, removing any skin and bones, and cut into small cubes. Dunk the tomatoes in boiling water, then peel and remove the seeds. Set in a colander for a few minutes to drain the excess water.

Pour a small amount of oil into nonstick pan and sauté the garlic over medium heat. Add the chili pepper and tomatoes, and mix. Lower the heat, then add the fish. Season with salt and simmer over low heat for five minutes. Check that the fish is completely cooked and the tomatoes are well blended in, then remove from heat, season with half the parsley, and cover.

In the meantime, cook the linguine in plenty of salted boiling water for the amount of time indicated on the package. Drain the pasta and pour into the pan with the seasoning, mix the ingredients evenly, and add 2 tablespoons of oil. Serve in dishes, garnishing and seasoning with the remaining parsley.

*This dish embodies all the exquisite simplicity of the Mediterranean diet: oil, nice ripe tomatoes, very fresh fish, and rapid cooking so that the few ingredients are well linked and taste their best. Of the long types of pasta, linguine are one of the best for fresh and light sauces. Furthermore the idealino chili pepper, from Calabria, has the perfect spiciness for combining with the decisive flavor of the amberjack. For preparing this linguine dish, the ingredients are key: they must be very fresh in order to develop the intense aromas characterizing the dish. Best accompanied with a white wine, such as a Grillo or a Vermentino.*

# SPICY CAVATELLI WITH OCTOPUS

Difficulty of preparation: Easy - Degree of difficulty: Easy - Preparation time: 30 minutes - Cooking time: 60 minutes - Resting time: 1 hour

## INGREDIENTS FOR 4 PEOPLE

3/4 LB (350 G) CAVATELLI-TYPE PASTA

4 TOMATOES, RIPE AND FIRM

1 3/4 LB (800 G) FRESH OCTOPUS

1 ONION

6 SPRIGS OF BASIL

1 FUEGUITOS CHILI PEPPER

EXTRA VIRGIN OLIVE OIL

WHOLE SEA SALT

Wash the octopus, remove the entrails and beak, then wash again. Cook in boiling water for 40 minutes, then let cool in its own cooking liquid. Meanwhile, immerse the tomatoes in boiling water for a minute, then peel and remove the seeds. Cut into small pieces and set in a colander to drain the excess liquid.

Peel the onion and cut into thin wedges. Heat 4 tablespoons of olive oil in a large nonstick pan and gently sauté the onions. When golden, add the chili pepper (left whole if you want to spice up the recipe without excess, or broken up into pieces, for a more pronounced flavor). Add the chopped tomato and cook until reduced by half. During the cooking, stir regularly and season with salt to taste. When the octopus has cooled to lukewarm, remove it from its cooking water and cut into small pieces. Add the octopus to the sauce and mix well so that the flavors blend evenly, simmering over low heat for 4-5 minutes and moistening, if necessary, with a few spoons of water from the cooking.

Just before cooking the pasta, trim the basil and chop half of it into pieces. Cook the cavatelli in plenty of salted boiling water, then drain and transfer into the pan with the sauce. Mix well and season with the chopped basil. Serve in plates, garnishing with whole basil leaves. Serve quite hot, for best appreciating the genuine scents of the sea and basil that will rise from the plate.

*Cavatelli are a traditional pasta originating from Molise and later spreading through Puglia, Calabria, and Campania. Its shape is perfect for collecting the sauce, and in this preparation it is obvious how suitable it is for absorbing and becoming enveloped with the seasoning. As for the cooking of the cavatelli, here is a suggestion for fans of decisive flavors: you can add some of the liquid from cooking the octopus into the water for cooking the pasta. The result will be a light pink color and an intense aroma. A young and light red wine or a rosé are an outstanding accompaniment for this very fragrant dish.*

# SPICY FREGOLA WITH SEAFOOD

Difficulty of preparation: Meduim · Degree of difficulty: Medium · Preparation time: 20 minutes · Cooking time: 20 minutes · Resting time: 2 hours

## INGREDIENTS FOR 4 PEOPLE

3/4 LB (350 G) SARDINIAN FREGOLA, MEDIUM SIZE

2 TO 2 1/2 LB (1 KG) CLAMS

2 CLOVES GARLIC

6 TBSP (90 G) CHOPPED TOMATOES

2 DRIED TOMATOES

1 DRIED IDEALINO CHILI PEPPER

1 FRESH DOLCEVITA CHILI PEPPER

3/4 OZ (20 G) PARSLEY

EXTRA VIRGIN OLIVE OIL

SALT

Wash the clams well, brushing them and discarding any empty shells, which fill with sand and must be eliminated. Soak the clams for a few hours in salted water, stirring from time to time. Then wash repeatedly in running water and drain. Let them open with dry heat (that is, without adding any condiment) in a pan, then after opening, remove and discard half the shells. Filter the water released from the clams, and keep aside until time for use. Set 4 cups (1 L) of salted water to boil in a pot.

Trim the parsley, wash, and pat dry with paper towels, then finely chop. Wash the chili peppers, then crumble the dried chili pepper and mince the fresh chili pepper. Peel the garlic and finely chop together with the dried tomatoes, then gently sauté the chili peppers, dried tomatoes, and garlic in 4 tablespoons of oil. When the garlic has turned nice and golden, add the clam nectar, the chopped tomatoes, and the chopped parsley (keeping aside a teaspoon of parsley for garnish).

Add the fregola to the cooking ingredients and pour in enough water to cover. Let cook for about 10 minutes, stirring from time to time, then correct for salt and adjust the heat so that the excess liquid of the seasoned pasta will absorb. Two minutes before completion of cooking, add the clams, stir, and season with the remaining parsley. Serve.

*Fregola, also spelled fregula, is a dried pasta typical of the Sardinian cuisine, made from durum wheat, and available in different sizes. The grains, slightly spherical in shape, recall couscous grains, of the homemade sort, that is, coarse and irregular. This marvelous foodstuff can be used in preparing soups based on meat broth, or with fish or seafood. The chili pepper makes an outstanding accompaniment to the inviting fragrance of this dish, and blends marvelously with the Mediterranean flavors of Sardinia. A dry white wine from the island, fresh and young, is the most suitable beverage for emphasizing its taste.*

# FAIRYTALE TABBOULEH

Difficulty of preparation: Easy - Degree of difficulty: Easy - Preparation time: 20 minutes - Cooking time: 5 minutes - Resting time: 4 minutes

## INGREDIENTS FOR 4 PEOPLE

14 OZ (400 G) PRE-COOKED COUSCOUS

4 TOMATOES

1 3/4 OZ (50 G) BLANCHED ALMONDS

4 CELERY STALKS

1 AZERBAIJAN CHILI PEPPER, POWDERED

1 GREEN HARISSA CHILI PEPPER

1 BUNCH ROCKET (ARUGULA) AND MINT

EXTRA VIRGIN OLIVE OIL

1 TBSP (14 G) CLARIFIED BUTTER

SALT

PEPPER

Coarsely chop half the almonds. Wash the vegetables. Cut the tomatoes into wedges and chop the celery into small pieces. Trim the rocket and the mint, then chop about 20 leaves of each. Wash the green chili pepper, chop into small pieces, and grind in a mortar.

Meanwhile, heat 1 2/3 cups (400 ml) water to boiling and salt to taste. Pour the couscous into a bowl, cover with the hot water, add the butter, and cover to let swell for the time indicated on the package. Stir well, separating the grains, and allow to cool.

Just before serving, combine the tomatoes, celery, almonds, and the chopped fresh herbs in a bowl. Correct for salt and pepper, and, if desired, add a drizzle of olive oil. Distribute the tabbouleh into the plates, then flavor with the powdered chili pepper and the remaining mint and rocket.

*Dedicated to the summer, tabbouleh is a refreshing dish that is easy to prepare, and nourishing as well as light. The fragrances of the herbs blend with the aroma of the grain in a triumph of flavor. There are many variations on seasonings for couscous that produce truly original salads. The semolina flour lends itself well to mixing with nearly any vegetable: you can add cucumbers, garlic, or onions, and naturally there must be some spices, in this dish so popular in the Middle Eastern cuisine. Its name derives from the Levantine Arabic tabbouleh, which signifies "medium spicy." In Syria it is served with mezes (starters) and garnished with lettuce. You can make the salad well in advance without having the tabbouleh loses its freshness; in fact, if left to rest for a few hours, the ingredients blend even better. Serve this salad with cold tea or with a young, light white wine.*

# ASIAN PASTA SALAD WITH PRAWNS, LIMES, AND FRAGRANT SPICES

*Difficulty of preparation: Medium - Preparation time: 30 minutes - Cooking time: 30 minutes - Resting time: 30 minutes*

## INGREDIENTS FOR 4 PEOPLE

1/2 LB (250 G) CHINESE VERMICELLI

16 PRAWNS

2 SCALLIONS, FINELY CHOPPED

20 BASIL LEAVES

1 LIME

2 TBSP (30 ML) SOY SAUCE

1 TBSP (15 ML) SESAME OIL

1 TBSP (14 G) CANE SUGAR

2 CLOVES GARLIC, CHOPPED

FRESH GINGER ROOT

2 CAYENNE CHILI PEPPERS

SALT

Wash the prawns and remove their shells. Place the shells in a pot with 2 cups of water and a pinch of salt. Boil for 30 minutes, then filter and reduce the liquid over high heat to obtain 3 1/2 tablespoons of concentrated fish broth. Bring 4 cups of water to a boil and immerse the shrimps until they just lose their transparency, about 30 seconds, then drain, cool under cold running water, and let rest together in a bowl with the cooled fish broth, to intensify their flavor. Heat about 1 L of water to boiling, place the vermicelli into a bowl, and cover with the boiling water. Let soften for 10 minutes, then drain.

Meanwhile, trim the basil. Wash the chili peppers and slice into rounds. Wash the spring onions, remove any tough outer leaves, finely slice, and place into a bowl. Pour in the oil, soy sauce, and the sugar, along with the sliced chili pepper rounds. Squeeze the lime. Wash and peel the ginger, then grate using an appropriate instrument (one allowing you to collect both the juice and the pulp). Now add all the other ingredients into the bowl. Peel the garlic, finely chop, and add into the marinade. Mix and let rest for 5 minutes.

At serving time, strain the marinade, then drain the pasta, pour into a bowl, add the prawns (eliminating the broth), pour in the seasoning sauce, and mix well to blend the flavors evenly. Serve in individual dishes, garnish with a few leaves of basil, and serve.

*Asian salad is a dish alternating the freshness of lime with the spiciness of red cayenne chili pepper. This dish is bursting with perfumes, and the various shades of the ingredients make it perfect for summer days. The freshness of the lime and the ginger harmonized well with the sweetness of the prawns, the pasta, and the sugar. The spicy note of the chili pepper completes this light and very inviting first course dish. A cool or warm green tea makes a perfect accompanying beverage for this pasta salad.*

# SPICY RICE SALAD
# WITH OCTOPUS AND OLIVES

*Degree of difficulty: Easy - Preparation time: 20 minutes - Cooking time: 40-50 minutes - Resting time: 1 hour*

## INGREDIENTS FOR 4 PEOPLE

1 3/4 LB (800 G) OCTOPUS

30 BLACK OLIVES, PITTED

9 OZ (250 G) RICE

2 STALKS CELERY

2 FRESH DADDY CHILI PEPPERS

2 LEMONS, ORGANICALLY GROWN

EXTRA VIRGIN OLIVE OIL

SALT

BLACK PEPPER

Wash the octopus, removing the entrails, beak, and eyes. Wash one of the lemons, cut into two, and place in a pot with 1 L (or 1 quart) of water. Bring to a boil and immerse the octopus. Let boil covered for 40 minutes, checking regularly that the water does not boil away. After this time, use a fork to test that the octopus is cooked; if needed, let cook for another 10 minutes. Turn off the heat, and let the octopus cool in its own cooking liquid. When cooled, drain, wash, and cut into pieces.

Boil the rice in 1 L (1 quart) of salted water, then drain, and pour into a bowl. Season with 2 tablespoons of olive oil so that the grains remain nicely separated from one another. Wash the chili peppers and cut into strips. Wash the celery and slice rather thinly. Cut the olives into rounds.

Pour the rice into a bowl along with the olives, the chili pepper, celery, and octopus. Season with freshly ground pepper and salt to taste, and 2 tablespoons of olive oil. Mix all the ingredients and, if desired, season with some freshly squeezed lemon juice.

*The flavors of this fresh dish of rice salad with octopus are not overwhelmed by the spiciness of the daddy chili pepper, rather they are surrounded by its stronger aroma. You can prepare the salad several hours before serving, presenting it as the first course or as a main course, along with another fresh vegetable salad. Cold jasmine tea or a chilled slightly fizzy white wine will emphasize the lightness of this dish, perfect for summer.*

# JAMBALAYA

*Difficulty of preparation: Medium - Degree of difficulty: Medium - Preparation time: 20 minutes - Cooking time: 20 minutes*

## INGREDIENTS FOR 4 PEOPLE

| | |
|---|---|
| 16 SHRIMP TAILS | 9 OZ (250 G) TOMATO PURÉE |
| 7 OZ (200 G) RICE, ROUND GRAIN | 1 TBSP (15 ML) TOMATO CONCENTRATE |
| 1 2/3 CUPS (400 ML) VEGETABLE BROTH | 3/4 OZ (20 G) PARSLEY |
| 1 ONION | 4 TBSP (60 ML) PALM OIL |
| 1 CLOVE GARLIC | 4 DROPS TABASCO SAUCE |
| 2 CELERY STALKS | 1 CLOVE |
| 1 SCOZZESE CHILI PEPPER | SALT |
| 2 RED DADDY CHILI PEPPERS | PEPPERCORNS |

Bring the broth to a boil and cook the rice, covered, over low heat for 10 to 15 minutes, depending on whether you prefer al dente or softer. Wash the Scotch bonnet chili pepper, removing seeds and stems, and finely chop. Peel the onion and garlic, and finely chop both. Wash the celery and cut into small chunks. Wash the chili peppers, removing stem, seeds, and white parts, then cut into thin strips. Pour half the oil into a nonstick pan and gently sauté the onion and garlic. When the onion has softened, add the vegetables (including the chili peppers), stir, and let cook over medium heat for 5 minutes.

Grind the clove, then add to the vegetable mixture along with the tomato purée and concentrate. Season with some freshly ground pepper and the Tabasco sauce, then stir thoroughly so that the flavors blend well. Remove the shells from the shrimp tails. In another nonstick pan, pour the remaining oil and quickly sauté the shrimps for just the amount of time needed for them to lose their natural transparency.

Trim the parsley, wash, and pat dry with paper towel; finely chop the leaves. Drain the rice, transfer into the pan with the vegetables, add the shrimps, season with salt to taste, stir carefully, and remove from the heat. Serve the Jambalaya in individual bowls, garnishing with the fresh parsley. The dish is also excellent served at room temperature.

*This preparation, originating in the Caribbean Islands, is extremely spicy and very aromatic: the Scotch bonnet chili pepper has a strong flavor, in fact, as well as a pronounced spiciness. It also perfectly fits all preparations made from fish and crustaceans. On the islands, it is accompanied with very cold beer, but a glass of dry white wine can also nicely emphasize the variety of scents and flavors in the dish.*

# SALMON RICE SEASONED WITH AJI

## INGREDIENTS FOR 4 PEOPLE

2/3 LB (300 G) RICE

7 OZ (200 G) FRESH SALMON FILLETS

14 OZ (400 G) FRESH PEAS

2 FRESH ORANGE AJI (OR AJI COLORADO) CHILI PEPPERS

1 SMALL ONION

3/4 OZ (20 G) CHIVES

EXTRA VIRGIN OLIVE OIL

SALT

Eliminate any bones, skin, and scales from the salmon. Wash the fillets and pat dry with paper towel, then cut the fillets into cubes. Peel the onion and thinly slice. Wash the chili peppers, remove the seeds and stems, and cut into small pieces. Shell the peas, wash, and let drain in a colander. Trim the chives, wash, and gently pat dry; cut half the chives into pieces. Bring a pot of salted water to a boil and cook the rice, covered, for 10-12 minutes (depending on how soft or chewy you like your rice; if you like it crunchier, remove from the heat earlier). Halfway through cooking, add the peas.

Meanwhile, pour 4 tablespoons olive oil into a nonstick pan and sauté the chili pepper and onion over high heat. When the onion begins to soften, add the salmon and cook for about 5 minutes over medium heat, or until it turns a nice even light pink color, stirring regularly so the salmon cooks uniformly.

Drain the rice and add to the salmon. Correct for salt and mix well to distribute the ingredients evenly. Sprinkle with the chopped chives. Serve in individual plates, decorating with the whole chives. Serve immediately.

*In this dish, which can be eaten either hot or cold, the medium spicy flavor of the aji chili pepper stands out marvelously, allowing those who are just new to approaching the world of chili peppers to enjoy without being overwhelmed. Compact and fleshy, the orange aji is also quite attractive, and lends itself well to various preparations. If you want to experiment with home cultivation, it is worth knowing that the plant is very adaptable and robust, and can even reach 2 m (2 yds) in height. A fruity and very fragrant white wine is the ideal complement for salmon rice seasoned with orange aji.*

# RICE WITH GARDEN FRESH FRAGRANCES

## INGREDIENTS FOR 4 PEOPLE

2/3 LB (300 G) RICE

3/4 OZ (20 G) CHIVES

3 SPRIGS FRESH MINT

3 SPRIGS FRESH MARJORAM

1 LEMON

1 AJI COLORADO CHILI PEPPER

1 DRIED CONQUISTADOR CHILI PEPPER

EXTRA VIRGIN OLIVE OIL

SALT

Clean and wash all the herbs, patting dry with kitchen cloth to remove any excess water. Remove the leaves of mint and marjoram from their stalks and finely chop half, together with half the chives. Wash the chili peppers and grind in a mortar. Pour the herbs and chili peppers into a bowl, season with 4 tablespoons of olive oil, and salt and pepper to taste.

Wash the rice in cold water until the water runs off transparent, then boil in a covered pot, with an equal amount of water. After about 8-10 minutes, the rice will have completely absorbed the water and its texture should be al dente. At this point, drain any excess water and transfer into the bowl with the herbs. Wash the lemon and cut into half; squeeze a few drops into the mixture and stir well. Correct for salt.

Just before serving, distribute the herbed rice into individual dishes and decorate with the remaining herbs and a slice of lemon.

*This dish is great whether consumed immediately, still slightly hot, or at room temperature. This rice can be seasoned and flavored depending on the aromatic bouquet you have available, but it is always better to try to use fresh, just gathered herbs rather than dried herbs. This is a first course dish that is not too filling, so it can be used to lighten the workload of the digestive system, taking advantage of the properties of the herbs and chili pepper, which are not only delicious but are also allies to our well-being. Indeed it is useful to remember that chili peppers stimulate the taste buds and the digestive process; mint promotes the secretion of bile; and marjoram normalizes intestinal functions, preventing any fermentation: so with this dish you can wish your dinner guests a buon appetito in a healthy manner! A mint infusion or green tea, unsweetened and served hot, make a fine complement to this dish.*

# SPICY ORANGE RICE

## INGREDIENTS FOR 4 PEOPLE

2/3 LB (300 G) RICE

2 ORANGES, ORGANICALLY GROWN

1 HABANERO CHILI PEPPER

1 SMALL ONION

3 1/3 OZ (100 ML) DRY WHITE WINE

2 CUPS (1/2 L) VEGETABLE BROTH

1 3/4 OZ (50 G) GRANA CHEESE, GRATED

2 TBSP (30 ML) EXTRA VIRGIN OLIVE OIL

BUTTER

SALT

Peel the onion and cut into very thin rounds. Wash the chili pepper and cut into halves; finely chop half the chili pepper and slice the other half into rounds. Attention: the habanero is very spicy, so avoid touching your face and carefully wash your hands after having handled it, if not using gloves. Wash the orange, remove the peel, taking care not to damage the white part, and cut into small thin strips. Press the juice, filter, and set aside until time for use. Peel the other orange and supreme the slices (that is, remove the white part and membrane from the wedges).

Heat the broth and keep warm until time for use. Grate the cheese and keep ready for use. In a pan, sauté the onion and the minced chili pepper in the oil along with the butter; when the onion begins to soften, add the rice and toast for about a minute, gently stirring. Add the orange juice and white wine. Raise the heat to high and allow the excess liquid to evaporate, stirring well so that the flavors blend. Add half the orange peel and, little by little as the rice absorbs the liquids, moisten with the broth, pouring in a ladleful at a time. Season with salt to taste during the cooking. Continue cooking over medium flame until the rice is cooked to the desired consistency, then stir in the cheese.

Serve the rice in individual bowls, each garnished with two slices of orange, a bit of the peel, and a few chili pepper rounds. This dish is excellent whether served freshly hot or at room temperature.

*This orange risotto dish is very fragrant and has a particular flavor, decidedly original. The habanero chili pepper, in addition to being very spicy, is equally aromatic and blends perfectly with the orange and the sweet flavor of the rice. The creaminess that develops from the cheese binds the ingredients, giving the dish an unforgettable flavor that is especially welcome in the warm months. Beer is the ideal beverage to accompany this risotto.*

# MEXICAN PAELLA

## INGREDIENTS FOR 4 PEOPLE

2/3 LB (300 G) RICE, PARBOILED

1/3 LB (150 G) CHICKEN BREAST

1/3 LB (150 G) PORK MEAT

3 1/2 OZ (100 G) MEXICAN BLACK BEANS, CANNED

5 OZ (140 G) CORN, STEAMED

7 OZ (200 G) RED BELL PEPPER

1 ONION

2 CLOVES GARLIC

1/5 TSP (0.15 G) SAFFRON

2 FRESH JALAPEÑO CHILI PEPPERS

1 GUAJILLO CHILI PEPPER IN BRINE

1/2 TSP (1 G) GROUND CURRY

1/2 TSP (1 G) GROUND CUMIN

3 1/3 OZ (100 ML) VEGETABLE BROTH

EXTRA VIRGIN OLIVE OIL

SALT

Drain the beans and rinse. Cut the chicken meat and pork meat into chunks. Peel the onion and garlic, then chop coarsely. Clean the guajillo and cut into rounds. Do the same with the jalapeños. Wash the bell peppers, remove the stems and seeds, then cut into strips. Drain the corn in a colander.

Warm the vegetable broth and dissolve the saffron in it. Wash the rice and let soak for 5 minutes, then drain. Pour 4 tablespoons olive oil into an iron skillet (ideal would be to use a paella pan). Sauté the garlic and onion, taking care they do not burn: keep the flame low and when they begin to turn golden and release their aromas, add the meats. Stir continually so that the meats cook uniformly, then cover and continue cooking for about 10 minutes before adding the rice. Now turn the heat to high and let the rice toast for about a minute, stirring continually. Add bell peppers, black beans, corn, and chili peppers. Season with cumin and coriander (dosing to your own preference), and season to taste.

Add the vegetable broth flavored with the saffron, then continue cooking, uncovered, over low heat until the rice is cooked to desired consistency. Gently stir from time to time so that the rice does not stick, and just before removing from the heat, correct for salt. Let the paella rest for a few minutes before serving.

*Mexican paella is a full meal in one course, flavorful, rich, and very tasty. This is one of the many variants on the classic Spanish paella: by contrast with its European relative, here the aromatic spicy flavor prevails, and more often than not, it is prepared without fish. The bright and warm colors make it a very lively dish and quite beautiful to behold. Mexican paella is excellent with very cold blond beer.*

# SPICY CREAM OF SQUASH AND CARROT SOUP

Difficulty of preparation: Easy - Degree of difficulty: Easy - Preparation time: 10 minutes - Cooking time: 30-40 minutes

## INGREDIENTS FOR 4 PEOPLE

1 LB (500 G) OF SQUASH

11 OZ (300 G) CARROTS

14 OZ (400 G) POTATOES

2 LEEKS

4 CUPS (1 L) VEGETABLE BROTH

3 DRIED BRITISH CHILI PEPPERS

EXTRA VIRGIN OLIVE OIL

SALT

Peel the squash, then remove the seeds and filaments; cut into small pieces. Wash and peel the carrots and potatoes; cut the carrots into rounds and the potatoes into small chunks. Remove the outer leaves, roots and green tips from the leeks, then slice. Heat the broth and keep warm until time for use.

Into a saucepan, pour 4 tablespoons of oil and sauté the leeks, the squash, the carrots, the chili peppers, crumbled into the pan, and the potatoes, for about 5 minutes over medium heat. After this time, add the vegetable broth, stir, correct for salt, cover the pan, and continue cooking for 20 to 25 minutes. Check that the vegetables are cooked to softness, then blend in a mixer. Return to the pan over low heat to continue thickening until the soup is dense and velvety, then remove from heat.

Serve the soup into individual bowls, decorated, if you wish, with a few pieces of squash (kept aside while blending the rest) or bread croutons.

*This creamy soup flavored with the British chili pepper is a light first course dish, very easy to prepare and very satisfying, especially in the autumn months, when the first cold days are beginning. The contrast between the sweetness of the squash and the spiciness of the chili pepper make this dish particularly appetizing. And besides, squash is a vegetable with many virtues: it is rich in beta-carotene and vitamin C, making it the perfect ally for facing the cold months. And as for vitamins, chili peppers themselves contain several, but particularly vitamin C: in fact it is the foodstuff that contains the highest quantity of vitamin C! A red wine, soft, light, and low in acid, makes an ideal accompaniment for this orange-colored cream of vegetable soup.*

# CICERI E TRIE
# (CHICKPEA AND PASTA SOUP)

## INGREDIENTS FOR 4 PEOPLE

11 OZ (300 G) CHICKPEAS

1 ONION

2 BAY LEAVES

1 SPRIG FRESH ROSEMARY

2 CONQUISTADOR CHILI PEPPERS

5 TBSP (75 ML) EXTRA VIRGIN OLIVE OIL

SALT

*FOR THE PASTA:*

9 OZ (250 G) DURUM WHEAT FLOUR

WATER, AS NEEDED

Soak the chickpeas for 10-12 hours, then rinse several times under running water and boil in 2 quarts of water, along with the bay leaves. Cook over low heat and salt to taste during cooking. On a comfortable working surface, pour the flour, making a well in the center. Into the well, pour half a glass of water, then blend the ingredients and knead, adding a spoonful of water from time to time as needed. After you have obtained a smooth mixture, roll it out into sheets about 1-2 mm thick. Flour the surface of the pasta sheet so that it does not stick, then roll it over on itself, making a roll. Now cut through the roll, forming ribbons that are about 3-4 mm wide and anywhere from 5-10 cm (2-4 inches) in length. Allow the ribbons of pasta to dry on a lightly floured kitchen cloth.

Wash the rosemary and remove the woody stem, retaining the leaves. Wash the chili peppers and slice into rounds. Peel the onion and cut into thin wedges, then sauté in a pan with the oil along with the rosemary and chili pepper. When the chickpeas are cooked, remove the bay leaves, reduce the cooking water, and keep warm.

Cook the trie pasta in salted boiling water, then drain. Sauté the pasta gently in the onion and herb mixture briefly to blend the flavors, then pour all into the broth with the chickpeas. Serve this soup of Ceci e Trie nice and hot.

*This highly nutritious and well-balanced soup dish, rich in essential amino acids, originates from the Italian peasant cuisine, more specifically, from Puglia and Basilicata. Usually we do not think about a dish from the point of view of its nutritional profile: rather we think of it as a pleasure at the end of a day of work or as an exploration of the territory. In reality, chickpeas and pasta can substitute meat outstandingly, providing the necessary amount of protein for our body. A full-bodied red wine makes a perfect accompaniment to this dish.*

# SPICY COCONUT-SHRIMP SOUP

## INGREDIENTS FOR 4 PEOPLE

1/3 LB (150 G) SHRIMP TAILS

1 1/4 CUPS (300 ML) NATURAL COCONUT MILK

1 BUNCH SPRING ONIONS

1 FRESH GINGER ROOT

2 CELERY STALKS, TENDER

2/3 LB (300 G) TOMATOES

2 FRESH ANDA CHILI PEPPERS

2 1/2 CUPS (600 ML) VEGETABLE BROTH

3 TBSP (45 ML) LIGHT SOY SAUCE

1 LEMON

2 TBSP (15 ML) PEANUT OIL

Remove the shells from the shrimps, leaving only the end part of the tail; immerse into boiling water for 30 seconds. Drain and pass under cold running water. Wash and peel the ginger, then mince using an appropriate utensil for collecting both juice and pulp.

Blanch and peel the tomatoes, remove the seeds, cut into small pieces, and let drain in a colander for five minutes. Press and filter the lemon juice. Clean the spring onions, removing the tough outer leaves, and slicing into rounds. Wash the celery and cut into small chunks. Clean the chili peppers using a moist cloth, and leave whole. Into a pot, pour 2 tablespoons of oil and sauté the onions over medium heat. Add a tablespoon of the ginger and its juice, the celery, chili peppers, and tomatoes. Stir well to blend the flavors, then add the coconut milk and the broth. Simmer over medium heat for 4 minutes, stirring regularly.

After this time, remove from the heat, add the shrimps (shrimps must cook for a very short time, otherwise they become hard), stir and season with the lemon juice and soy sauce. Serve the soup in individual bowls. If you like, you can decorate with a few pieces of onion stalk and a few chili peppers (if not crumbled or broken, the chili peppers will not release their spiciness into the soup).

*This soup, originally from Thailand, creates a wonderful contrast of sweet and spicy. It can be served either hot or at room temperature. You can also enrich it by accompanying with a bit of white rice: in this case it is advisable to let the broth reduce. In this recipe, the chili pepper succeeds in exalting the sweetness of the coconut and is intentionally left whole, so as to just barely emphasize, with an aromatic note, the softness and sweetness of the soup. A cup of green tea makes an ideal beverage to accompany this dish.*

# SEAFOOD STEW

## INGREDIENTS FOR 4 PEOPLE

5 MULLETS

5 MANTIS SHRIMP

5 LANGOUSTINES

5 SHRIMP

14 OZ (400 G) SQUID RINGS

9 OZ (250 G) MOSCARDINI (THE *ELEDONE MOSCHATA*, OR MUSKY OCTOPUS, FROM THE MEDITERRANEAN)

1 LB (500 G) MUSSELS

2/3 LB (300 G) CLAMS

1 CUP (250 ML) WHITE WINE

1/2 OZ (15 G) HERBS, E.G., OREGANO, ROSEMARY, THYME

3/4 OZ (20 G) FRESH PARSLEY

1 ONION

2 CLOVES GARLIC

2 IDEALINO CHILI PEPPERS

EXTRA VIRGIN OLIVE OIL

8 SLICES WHITE BREAD

SALT

Wash the mussels and clams, removing any impurities from the shells using a metal brush. Leave them to soak in salted water for 2 hours, then drain. Wash the mullets and squids under running water and remove the dark outer film from the moscardini. Wash the langoustines, the shrimp, and the mantis shrimp; on each of these, make an incision from head to tail so that they open more easily when cooked. Wash the herbs, keeping the parsley aside. Peel the garlic and onion. Coarsely chop the onion. Pour 4 cups of water into a pot to prepare a broth; add 1 mullet, 1 mantis shrimp, 1 langoustine, 1 shrimp, 1 clove garlic, 1 onion, and the herbs. Let boil for about 30 minutes, then filter and salt to taste.

Toast the bread in the oven at 425° F (220° C) for 5 minutes, then let cool at room temperature. Trim the parsley and finely chop. Wash and slice the chili peppers.

In a large nonstick pan, pour 4 tablespoons of olive oil, the remaining garlic, freshly crushed, the chili peppers, half the parsley, the mussels, and clams. Stir and let cook over high heat for 2 minutes. Salt to taste. Add the squids and moscardini, then let cook for another 2 minutes. Now add the shrimp, langoustines, mantis shrimp, and finally, the mullets, flavoring with the white wine. Let the mixture reduce over high heat, stirring continually. Pour in the fish broth and remove from the heat. Place 2 slices of bread, 1 mullet, 1 shrimp, 1 langoustine, and 1 mantis shrimp on each plate, and then pour the broth with the seafood and other ingredients over everything. Garnish with the remaining parsley and, if you wish, add a few drops of oil. Serve quite hot.

*This delicious first course dish is typical of central Italy, but it can also prove to be an entirely valid main course dish. The ingredients follow the seasons and what the fisherman's catch has to offer. A good full-bodied Sauvignon makes an ideal accompaniment for the dish.*

# "SPECIAL" BOUILLABAISSE

Difficulty of preparation: Difficult - Degree of difficulty: Medium-Difficult - Preparation time: 40 minutes - Cocking time: 50 minutes

## INGREDIENTS FOR 4 PEOPLE

3 1/3 LB (1.5 KG) MIXED FISH, SUCH AS JOHN DORY,
    GURNARD, WEEVER OR SPIDER FISH, CONGER EEL,
    RASCASSE, WRASSE
1 CARROT
3 ONIONS
2 CLOVES GARLIC
3 FRESH TOMATOES
3/4 OZ (20 G) CHOPPED PARSLEY
1 TBSP (5 G) FRESH WILD FENNEL

1 TBSP (5 G) CHOPPED THYME
1/5 TSP (0.15 G) SAFFRON
1 YELLOW BELL PEPPER
1 LADLE OF BROTH
1 CUP (250 ML) DRY WHITE WINE
EXTRA VIRGIN OLIVE OIL
2 DELICATO CHILI PEPPER
8 SLICES OF BREAD
SALT, PEPPER

Peel the tomatoes, remove the seeds, and cut into small pieces. Wash the yellow bell pepper, remove the stem and seeds, then cut into cubes. Peel the carrot and boil it, then smash into a purée. Peel and chop the onions; peel and crush the garlic; place these into a rather large pot along with the fennel, the carrot purée, and the chili peppers, freshly chopped. Add a few tablespoons olive oil and sauté over low heat. Add the chopped tomatoes and bell pepper. Stir using a wooden spoon, season with salt and pepper to taste. Add in the white wine and allow to evaporate.

Wash and clean the fish, removing the entrails and any bones from the fillets. Add these into the sauce, lowering the heat to minimum. Dissolve the saffron in a ladle full of broth and pour into the pot. Let cook for about 30 minutes, stirring regularly. Watch to see that the sauce does not reduce too much; if necessary, add a ladle full of hot water when necessary. Collect the fish using a slotted spoon, then remove their bones, heads, and tails; mash the heads and tails with a fork and return to the broth, adding also the fillets. Let cook for 10 minutes. Just before removing from the heat, toast the bread.

When cooked, distribute the soup in individual bowls, making sure that each diner also receives some pieces of whole fish. Garnish with parsley and, if you desire, some freshly ground pepper. Dip the slices of bread into the bouillabaisse and serve quite hot.

*Originally from French cuisine, this delicious recipe combines textures that are different but harmonious with each other. Very fragrant and aromatic, bouillabaisse is a dish with a robust flavor, best appreciated in countries bordering on the coast. Best enjoyed with a dry full-bodied white wine.*

# CHINESE BEEF FANTASY
# WITH PASTA AND VEGETABLES

## INGREDIENTS FOR 4 PEOPLE

2/3 LB (300 G) BEEF CUT (A SINGLE PIECE)

7 OZ (200 G) CHINESE EGG PASTA

1 FRESH AZERBAIJAN CHILI PEPPER

3 CLOVES GARLIC

1 CAN BABY CORN COBS

1 RED BELL PEPPER, NOT SPICY

2 SPRING ONIONS WITH PLENTY OF NICE GREEN LEAVES

3 TBSP (45 ML) SOY SAUCE

1 TBSP (15 G) MUSTARD SEEDS

2 CUPS (500 ML) BROTH

2 TBSP (30 ML) SOYBEAN OIL

SALT

PEPPERCORNS

Cook the pasta in plenty of salted boiling water, following the cooking time indicated on the package, then drain. Cool under cold running water to halt the cooking, then drain once again. Cover and set aside until time for use. Heat the broth and keep warm, ready for use. Trim and wash the spring onions, then cut into rounds, including the green parts. Cut the meat into thin slices. Wash the chili pepper, remove the stem and seeds, then finely chop. Peel and cut the garlic into thin slices. Drain the corn cobs of their canning liquid and rinse under running water. Wash the bell pepper, remove the stem and seeds, and cut into rounds.

Pour 2 tablespoons of the oil into a saucepan and, over high heat, sauté the mustard seed, garlic, and chili pepper, then add the bell pepper and meat. Lower the flame, salt to taste, and flavor with some freshly ground pepper. Stir repeatedly so that the ingredients are uniformly cooked. Add the broth and soy sauce, then cover and let simmer for 4 minutes. Add the corn cobs and spring onions, then continue cooking for another 3-4 minutes. Lastly, add the pasta, stirring well to evenly distribute the various ingredients.

You can either transfer the Fantasy soup into a serving bowl for service at the table, or serve directly in single portion bowls. Serve immediately to best appreciate the inviting perfumes.

*The Chinese are masters at preparing tasty soups. The various colors are the first suggestion emanating from the bowl, then come the perfumes, and lastly, the palette is rewarded with a kaleidoscope of flavors. This tasty soup is ideal for cold day and makes a complete meal. It can be appreciated with jasmine scented green tea, or, for wine lovers, we can suggest a glass of young and light red wine, such as a Novello.*

# SPICY SOUP WITH QUESADILLAS

Difficulty of preparation: Medium - Degree of difficulty: Medium - Preparation time: 20 minutes - Cooking time: 45 minutes

## INGREDIENTS FOR 4 PEOPLE

**FOR THE SOUP:**

14 OZ (400 G) SPICY BEANS, CANNED
6 1/3 CUPS (1 1/2 L) VEGETABLE BROTH
1/2 CUP (125 ML) SHERRY
2 ONIONS
2 CLOVES GARLIC
2 TBSP (15 ML) OLIVE OIL
1 TBSP (15 G) GROUND CUMIN
1 BAY LEAF
SALT AND PEPPER

**FOR THE SAUCE AND TORTILLAS:**

5 OZ (150 G) SOUR CREAM
7 OZ (200 G) TOMATOES
2 TBSP (2 G) CHOPPED FRESH CILANTRO LEAVES
7 OZ (200 G) MOZZARELLA
1 CHILI DE ONZA CHILI PEPPER
2 TBSP (10 G) DRIED JALAPEÑO CHILI PEPPER
2 SPRING ONIONS
4 WHEAT TORTILLAS

Wash the chili pepper, remove the stem and seeds, then cut into small pieces. Pour the sour cream into a container and add the chili and half the chopped cilantro leaves. Leave this mixture to rest in the refrigerator until time for use. Peel the garlic and finely chop; peel the onions and coarsely chop. In a nonstick pan, heat 2 tablespoons of the oil and gently sauté the onion. When soft, add the garlic, cumin, and the bay leaf, carefully stirring so that the flavors blend well. Add the beans and the broth, then let simmer over low heat for 20 minutes, stirring regularly. After this time, remove some of the beans (drained) and set aside whole. Add the sherry to the soup then blend in the mixer until creamy. Return the soup to the pan, adding also the whole beans, and continue cooking for 15 minutes, stirring from time to time and seasoning as needed with salt and pepper to taste.

Pour the soup into a bowl. Cut the mozzarella into small cubes and keep 4 pieces apart for garnishing. Wash the tomatoes, remove the seeds, and cut into small pieces. Trim the spring onions, wash, and slice into rounds (both white and green parts), then add these to the mozzarella in a bowl. Season with the jalapeño chili pepper, crumbled, and the chili de onza, and carefully mix the ingredients.

When time to serve, heat a nonstick skillet and place one of the tortillas into it. Cover this with the cheese stuffing and top with another tortilla, making a quesadilla. Let cook for a few minutes, then remove the quesadilla and cut into four parts. Repeat this process until all the ingredients have been used. When serving at the table, for each diner, prepare a small tray with a bowl of soup, decorated with one of the mozzarella chunks, some fresh chili pepper, and some chopped cilantro leaves, and beside this, the sour cream in a small cup, and pieces of quesadilla.

*This dish contains all the aromas and flavors of Mexico. Very tasty and nutritious, it is a traditional recipe taking inspiration from the peasant cuisine. It makes a complete meal, one where freshness and spiciness alternate mouthful after mouthful. Beer makes the ideal beverage to best accompany the fresh flavors of this bean soup with quesadillas.*

# THAI STYLE CHICKEN SOUP

## INGREDIENTS FOR 4 PEOPLE

1 LB (500 G) CHICKEN BREAST

1 2/3 CUPS (400 ML) COCONUT MILK

2 CUPS (500 ML) CHICKEN BROTH

1 MEDIUM LEEK

1 CLOVE GARLIC

2 INDIANO CHILI PEPPER, FRESHLY CHOPPED

1 TSP (2 G) POWDERED CURRY

1 TBSP (15 G) GROUND CUMIN

1 TSP (2 G) GROUND CORIANDER SEEDS

1 STALK LEMONGRASS

2 TSP (11 G) SAMBAL OELEK CHILI PASTE

1 TBSP (8 G) CORNSTARCH

1 TSP (5 ML) FISH SAUCE

1 TSP (5 ML) LIME JUICE

2 TBSP (30 ML) PEANUT OIL

SALT

Remove any bones and fatty parts from the chicken, then cut into cubes. Wash and slice the lemongrass. Wash the leek, removing the outer leaves and green tips, and finely slice. Heat the chicken broth and keep warm until time for use. Sift the cornstarch into the fish sauce, and stir with a whisk. Add a few tablespoons of broth, as needed, and work the mixture until smooth and even.

Heat the oil in a pot large enough to contain all the ingredients. Sauté the leek, the clove of garlic, lemon grass, and chili pepper. Add the chicken, then add salt and flavor with the curry, cumin, and powdered coriander. Mix all ingredients and let cook until the chicken is cooked to an even color, then add the chicken broth, the coconut milk, and the sambal oelek. Let simmer over low heat, uncovered, for about 10 minutes, then add the lime juice and cornstarch sauce, mixing well to blend.

Remove from the heat, correct for salt, and transfer into individual bowls for serving. This recipe is excellent whether hot or warm.

*The highly aromatic ingredients with there pronounced personalities make this soup a very interesting sensory experience. The dish – fresh, articulate, and very rich – presents exotic and unusual flavors to the palette. It is particularly suitable for hot days: despite the "fire" of the chili peppers, the dish is easily digestible and not heavy. It can be accompanied by a freshly squeezed fruit juice, such as iced water with a bit of lime, or with a very cold, lightly alcoholic beer.*

# MAIN COURSES

n most of the world, a main dish is delicious and nutritious: meat or fish, usually accompanied by vegetables and grains. Spices, aromas and colors differentiate preparations from country to country. Climates and temperatures are often what cause the differences in the approach to food. If the chili, at one time, was also used to preserve food, it goes without saying that in hot and humid regions it was necessary, as well as pleasurable, since food was cooked with liberal doses of chili pepper. Conversely, in cold countries, its use is less widespread. This statement does not apply to goulash, a tasty preparation of Hungarian origin, in which the main ingredient is chili in the form of paprika. It can be spicy or sweet, depending on the pepper used and whether both the seeds and the innards were removed or ground entirely. The herbs and spices are the precise elements that can transform dishes. Take prawns, for example. We can prepare them with orange, inspired by the recipes of southern Italy, and boil them down with a hint of suavito chili. Or the Mexican way with a habanero sauce, or the recipe with mint, yogurt and cherry peppers. Crustaceans vary slightly in their flavor, but change remarkably thanks to the sauce and spices used; each case makes the difference from mildly spicy to fiery hot! And as for pork? In South America it is prepared with fruit and acrobata chili pepper rings, yet the same kind of meat in Thailand takes on a different nuance of flavor that is completely different thanks to namesake chili and lime juice. At the table, it would be nice to shut off the mind as to not affect the palate, being free to travel within the flavors without paying attention to habits, maintaining only the curiosity of a continuous discovery played on a global scale.

Each country, within its food traditions, tells its own history, and food is a way to get to the heart of the local uses and customs. Like in Mexico, the strength of the hot sun seems to be contained in powerful habanero and jalapeño peppers, always used to make the table as fiery as the land; the dishes, in fact, have a special potency, of which the chili is an excellent example. Preparations based on beans and meat seasoned with a mix of some of the most powerful peppers, such as the jalapeño, poblano and conquistador, or fajitas accompanied by the equally fiery tabasco pepper.

In Italy, each region tells its story: on the island Campana di Ischia, for example, we find the Ischia style rabbit, whose recipe belongs to the peasant tradition. It is a dish that resembles the sun, in which tomatoes and herbs from the garden, together with *salamandra* peppers, are wrapped with the tender meat, thus making it lightly tasty and fragrant.

In India, where everything is colorful, the dishes speak this language of color with bright tones from nature that come alive on the table. From meat to chicken, it is clear that after marinating in a base of herbs and spices, the food lights up like a fiery sunset, enriched with scarlet shades that have been infused into the meat thanks to the marinating sauce, and subsequently ignites the palate. Prepare a chicken with ginger, turmeric, coconut and almonds. A wonderful set of flavors that further enhances the meat of this farmyard animal and turns it into a tasty and very delicious dish are the spicy notes of the aromatic *naga morich* and *cabe besar* chili peppers. From India, let's move on to North Africa to appreciate the Maghreb lamb, a combination of intense and aromatic flavors from the coriander and cumin (both equally enveloping and penetrating aromas), underlined by the presence of soft *aci sivri* pepper and contrasted by the sweetness of candied lemons.

# BEEF AND PEPPER
# FAJITAS WITH TORTILLAS

*Difficulty of preparation: Easy - Degree of difficulty: Easy - Preparation time: 20 minutes - Cooking time: 20 minutes*

## INGREDIENTS FOR 4 PEOPLE

1 LB (500 G) TENDER LEAN BEEF

8 READY-MADE TORTILLAS

1 RED BELL PEPPER

1 YELLOW BELL PEPPER

1 GREEN BELL PEPPER

1 PINCH OREGANO

2 TBSP (30 ML) OLIVE OIL

1 TSP (2 G) POWDERED TABASCO CHILI

SALT

PEPPERCORNS

6 3/4 OZ (200 G) SPICY MEXICAN-STYLE
  TOMATO SAUCE

CILANTRO

Cut the beef into strips about 1 cm wide and 5.6 cm long. Wash the peppers and cut in half, then remove the seeds and white innards and cut it into strips.

Heat the olive oil in a frying pan. On high heat, sear the beef and the peppers, and then continue cooking over medium heat for 5 to 7 minutes. Generously season with salt, freshly ground pepper, the chili pepper and oregano. Meanwhile, preheat the oven to 480° F (250° C) and bake the tortillas for a few minutes, then remove them and keep them covered with a towel to keep them hot and soft.

When the meat and peppers are at the desired consistency, remove them from the stove, stuff the tortillas and serve accompanied with the spicy tomato sauce, chili and cilantro.

*Meat fajitas are a traditional Mexican recipe that has spread all over the globe because of its simplicity and goodness, as well as how easy it is to prepare such as satisfying and very tasty dish. While cooking, you can also add chopped tomatoes to obtain a softer consistency that binds well to the other ingredients. If you want to experience a particular addition to this very appetizing dish, you can marinate the meat in tequila. Cold blond beer or smooth tequila, the choice is yours!*

# CHILI WITH MEAT
# AND THREE PEPPERS

Difficulty of preparation: Medium - Degree of difficulty: Medium - Preparation time: 20 minutes - Cooking time: 2 hours - Soaking time: 10-12 hours

## INGREDIENTS FOR 4 PEOPLE

14 OZ (400 G) BEEF

3 1/2 OZ (100 G) ONION

1 POBLANO CHILI PEPPER

1 JALAPEÑO CHILI PEPPER

4 POWDERED CONQUISTADOR CHILI PEPPERS

5 1/4 OZ (150 G) DRIED BLACK BEANS

9 OZ (250 G) TOMATO PULP

1 CLOVE GARLIC

1 TSP (2 G) GROUND CUMIN

EXTRA VIRGIN OLIVE OIL

SALT

Let the black beans soak overnight in cold water, then drain, rinse and pour into a saucepan with about 2 cups of water. Boil for 10 minutes, drain and remove the cooking water (which makes them particularly digestible), pour into another pot with boiling water and simmer while covered over low heat for about 1 hour and a half. Stir occasionally and salt to taste.

In the meantime, peel the onion and the garlic and chop them finely. Wash the peppers, remove the stem, the white insides and seeds then cut into small pieces. Cut the beef into cubes. Dissolve the cumin and chili powder in a glass of hot water. In a non-stick pan, pour two tablespoons of oil and fry the onion and garlic. When the former have softened, add the pepper and stir, then add the meat, stir again and cook evenly for 5 minutes. Once the meat is golden, pour in the tomato pulp, add more salt if needed, add the water with cumin and chili and cook covered on low heat for about 1 hour. Check regularly and, if necessary add warm water.

When done, drain the cooked beans and add them to the meat, stir and continue cooking for another 20 minutes, adding, if necessary, a ladle of hot water. Serve the *chili con carne* fresh off the stove, decorate it with fresh jalapeño and accompany this dish with hot tortillas.

*The* chili con carne *is a dish for palates accustomed to spicy foods. Though it is a very common dish in the United States, its origin is attributed to Mexico. Chili purists debate whether or not to use meat, tomatoes and various spices in the creation of the recipe, as in reality it should simply be a plate of beans served with a sauce made of peppers. Compared to the original version, our dish is enriched with both ingredients and both aromas and is very appetizing: you are sure to have an intense experience! A clear, light and fresh beer would be the ideal drink.*

# TWO-COLORED ROAST

## INGREDIENTS FOR 4 PEOPLE

10 1/2 OZ (300 G) COOKED ROAST

7 OZ (200 G) WHITE RICE

2/3 LB (300 G) GREEN BEANS

4 FIRM, RIPE TOMATOES

4 SMALL ALFIERE CHILI PEPPERS

1 WHITE ONION

1/2 GLASS DRY WHITE WINE

1 CUP (236 ML) VEGETABLE BROTH

3 1/2 TBSP (50 G) BUTTER

2 TBSP (30 ML) OIL

1 CLOVE GARLIC

1/2 TSP (1 G) GROUND CUMIN

SALT

Trim the beans by removing the ends of the pods, put them in cold water for 5 minutes, then rinse and drain them. Next, peel the onion and slice thinly, peel the garlic and chop finely, remove the stalk and seeds from chilies, then wash and slice them.

Wash the rice several times in running water and then boil covered on low heat in a quantity of water equal to its volume. After about 8-10 minutes, remove from heat and mix in two tablespoons of olive oil so that the grains do not stick together. Let cool at room temperature. Wash the tomatoes, cut into wedges and remove the seeds and then let the excess water drain in a colander. In a non-stick pan, melt the butter and fry the onion and garlic. To this add the chili, green beans and tomatoes then add the wine and cook for 5 minutes on high heat.

Meanwhile, fray the meat and add to the pan with the other ingredients. Stir to blend the flavors and leave on the stove for about 15 minutes, basting with broth as needed. During this last cooking stage, add cumin and salt to taste. When finished, remove from heat, place the rice in individual bowls, join the meat to the vegetables and serve immediately.

*This dish from the island of Cuba is an excellent second course, but can also be a main dish for a full meal. White rice is wonderfully accompanied by the vegetables flavored with chili, which you can add at will. For a less spicy mixture, you can leave it in whole. It is an ideal recipe to turn a leftover roast into something very tasty; giving it a delicious personality and making it beautiful to behold. A glass of full-bodied red wine or of dark beer is the ideal drink with which to accompany this tasty preparation.*

# COCONUT STEW

## INGREDIENTS FOR 4 PEOPLE

1 3/4 LB (800 G) TENDERLOIN

1 LARGE ONION (ABOUT 200 G)

6 CLOVES GARLIC

1 CAYENNE CHILI PEPPER

6 CURRY LEAVES

3 TBSP (45 ML) COCONUT OIL

5 TBSP (31.5 G) CURRY POWDER

6.75 FL. OZ (200 ML) COCONUT CREAM

13.50 FL. OZ (400 ML) COCONUT MILK

SALT

Wash the peppers and cut into rings. Eliminate any loose fat and sinew from the meat then cut into small cubes. Peel the onion and cut into thin slices, peel the garlic and freshly crush, then fry both in the oil in a large pot with high sides. Finally, add the curry leaves and chili. Cook over medium heat until the onion become golden.

Boil 4 cups of water and leave on the stove until needed for use. To the pan, add the beef, curry powder, coconut milk and a pinch of salt. Cover the ingredients with water and cook over low heat until the meat becomes tender. While this is cooking, add salt to taste and stir occasionally.

If necessary, pour more hot water in. After about 40 minutes, try the consistency to make sure it is to your liking. If it is indeed to your liking, remove from heat, season with the coconut cream, and serve the stew hot. Accompany with white rice, unleavened bread or boiled potatoes.

*The traditional cuisine of the Maldives is based mainly on fish and local produce. There we find an abundance of coconut, which is used either in its juice, cream or pulp form. The dishes are often flavored with spices and made spicy with chili that through its fiery intensity seems to aid in bearing the heat of the environment. Meat is also an important specialty that is wonderfully combined with sweet fruit. Having the fortune of finding oneself on one of the beautiful Maldivian islands and trying the local cuisine, one can enjoy the stew along with non-alcoholic beverages such as fruit juice or the unavoidable coconut milk. Repeating this undertaking at home is very easy and the flavor is very interesting because it harmonizes the sweetness of the coconut, the sapidity of the meat and the spiciness of the chili. The other spices envelope the stew and offer wonderful fragrances. A medium strength red beer is the perfect drink with which to accompany the coconut stew.*

# GOULASH

Difficulty of preparation: Medium - Degree of difficulty: Medium - Preparation time: 20 minutes - Cooking time: 2.30 hours

## INGREDIENTS FOR 4 PEOPLE

1 3/4 LB (800 G) LEAN BEEF

1 TBSP (7 G) PAPRIKA

1 DRIED AND POWDERED VIGEI
   CHILI PEPPER

2 BIG ONIONS

1 PINCH GROUND CUMIN

3 1/2 OZ (100 G) TOMATO PULP

1 GLASS RED WINE

1 CLOVE GARLIC

1 TSP (2 G) CHOPPED MARJORAM

WHITE FLOUR

2 CUPS (1/2 L) BEEF BROTH

EXTRA VIRGIN OLIVE OIL

SALT AND PEPPER

Put the broth to a boil and keep warm until ready to use. Remove any excess fat from the beef, cut into cubes and pass them through the flour. Peel the onions and garlic, chop finely and brown in two tablespoons of olive oil in a nonstick saucepan. When they are golden, add the meat and let brown on moderate heat for about 10 minutes. Add salt to taste and pour in the red wine.

Add cumin powder, paprika, marjoram leaves, powdered chili and tomato to the mixture. Add pepper to taste. Cook over low heat for 10 minutes and then pour in the broth. Cover and simmer on medium heat for about 2 hours, stirring occasionally and checking from time to time if it is necessary to add more broth.

At the end, make sure that the meat is of a desired consistency; if not then continue cooking to your liking. The sauce should thicken and bind into an enveloping and very tasty gravy. Serve the goulash piping hot with boiled potatoes or with traditional Hungarian dumplings made of white flour, as well as with bread or boiled vegetables.

*This dish of Hungarian origin is extremely tasty and very fragrant with the eye-catching color and outstanding aroma of paprika, not to mention the unmistakable flavor of the chili pepper, all which makes this dish memorable. This recipe, now "cleared through customs, has become a widespread preparation on an international scale. It is fairly easy to prepare but requires time and attention in order to get the best results. A full-bodied red, with a robust personality, is the perfect companion for this dish of intense aromas and flavors.*

# BALINESE CHICKEN WINGS

## INGREDIENTS FOR 4 PEOPLE

12 CHICKEN WINGS

4 CLOVES GARLIC

1 DRIED CABE BESAR CHILI PEPPER

6 DUE MORI CHILI PEPPERS

1 ONION

1 TBSP (7 G) TURMERIC

1 TSP (2 G) BROWN SUGAR

EXTRA VIRGIN OLIVE OIL

WHOLE SEA SALT

Separate the wings dividing them at the joints and eliminate any excess parts. Pass them over a flame so that any reaming smaller feathers are eliminated. Then wash and dry them.

Crush the dried chili in a mortar. Peel the onion and garlic and chop both finely. Prepare the marinade by mixing the dried chili, onion and garlic with turmeric, salt, pepper, sugar and two tablespoons of olive oil.

Dip the wings in the marinade, having it bind to the mixture, and let stand for 2 hours. When the time comes for preparing the dish, preheat the oven to 390° F (200° C) and a cover a baking tray with a sheet of waxed paper. Spread the chicken pieces onto the paper and pour the remaining marinade over them. Bake for 30 minutes and then remove from the oven. Spread the chicken wings on a platter and decorate with fresh chili peppers, so that they may be useful to further flavor the dish, at the discretion of the individual diner. Serve hot.

*This dish is very tasty. The contrast between the sweetness and softness of the meat and the crust that is created during baking, as well as the ease of preparation and availability of the ingredients, make it a delicacy for everyone. This recipe, originally from Bali, is part of the home kitchen: the chicken is a domesticated animal widespread throughout the island, especially in rural areas, and is usually served with the inevitable boiled rice that tempers the strength of the chili. Excellent as a second course, this recipe is also perfect as an appetizer, or as an original snack. It is a very informal dish to be enjoyed with your hands! A clear and well-chilled beer would be the ideal drink, but if you wish to savor this dish the Balinese way, try with an iced lime juice or a pineapple smoothie.*

# KUNG PAO

## INGREDIENTS FOR 4 PEOPLE

1 3/4 LB (800 G) CHICKEN BREAST

3 FRESH BELVIOLA CHILI PEPPERS

1 3/4 OZ (50 G) TOASTED PEANUTS

3 TBSP (45 ML) PEANUT OIL

SALT

*FOR THE SAUCE:*

1 GREEN ONION

2 CLOVES GARLIC

2 TBSP (30 ML) CHICKEN BROTH

2 TBSP (30 ML) SAKE

1 TBSP (15 ML) SOY SAUCE

1 TBSP (15 ML) WHITE WINE VINEGAR

2 TSP (8 G) SUGAR

1 TBSP (15 ML) SESAME OIL

Clean the chicken by removing any fat, bones and skin and then cut it into cubes. Cut the peppers in half lengthwise and remove seeds and stems. Trim and wash the onion, then chop finely into rings starting with the white end and finishing with the green end. Peel and chop the garlic.

Heat a wok, pour in the oil and on a high flame sauté the peppers for a few seconds, then remove them from the oil and set aside, you will need them later. In the same frying oil, throw in the chicken and peanuts and sauté for 5 minutes, stirring constantly. Add salt to taste, then remove from wok and transfer it into a bowl.

Prepare the sauce by pouring all the ingredients (except the sesame oil and the green parts of the onion) into the wok and bring to a boil. Stir consistently and after 2 minutes incorporated the chicken with peanuts and chilies, then cook for another 4 minutes. At the end, season with sesame oil and the small pieces of onion, mix together and transfer into individual bowls. Serve at once.

*This dish of Chinese origin, which often figures on the menu in the correct modern transliteration (Gong Bao), is extremely appetizing thanks to the richness of the sauce that is seasoned with chicken and peanuts. It can also be made with duck or with a whole chicken that has been cut into pieces. Characteristic of this very nice and delicious second course dish are the contrasts, such as the one between the soft tenderness of the meat and the crunchy texture of the peanuts. It can be accompanied with boiled white rice, served at room temperature, or with slices of toasted bread. A very cold Chinese lager, or a young red wine that is fresh and light tasting, are the most suitable drinks for Kung Pao.*

# CHICKEN KORMA

Difficulty of preparation: Medium - Degree of difficulty: Medium - Preparation time: 20 minutes - Cooking time: 30-40 minutes - Resting time: 12 hours

## INGREDIENTS FOR 4 PEOPLE

1 1/3 LB (600 G) CHICKEN BREAST

1 TBSP (6 G) FRESHLY GRATED GINGER

1 CLOVE GARLIC, MINCED

2 OZ (50 G) THICK YOGURT

1 DRIED NAGA MORICH CHILI PEPPER

1 FRESH CABE BESAR CHILI PEPPER

1 FRESH GREEN CHILI PEPPER

1 ONION

1 PINCH GARAM MASALA

1 PINCH TURMERIC

1 PINCH GROUND BLACK PEPPER

1 FRESH COCONUT

1 TBSP (9 G) CHOPPED ALMONDS

1 LEMON

WATER

OIL

SALT

Cut the chicken breast into cubes, removing any loose fat, skin or bones, then place in a container and pour the chopped ginger, garlic and yogurt on top. Cover with plastic wrap and let stand overnight in the refrigerator. When it's time to prepare the dish, peel the onion, cut into pieces and in a blender liquefy with the naga morich chili and 2 tablespoons of water until the mixture is smooth and well blended. Break the coconut and collect the juice, then grate a quarter of the fruit and keep aside until needed.

In a pan, pour in two tablespoons of olive oil and spices (garam masala, turmeric and pepper). Heat and mix everything together for 30 seconds, add the onion and pepper cream, then turn up the heat and add the chicken with the marinade. Cook for about 10 minutes then add the grated coconut and two tablespoons of coconut juice. Mix well and continue cooking for about 30 minutes while stirring occasionally. Make sure that the sauce does not congeal: in case it does, you can add more water or coconut juice.

Once cooked, season with salt. Add the finely ground almonds and, if desired, a few drops of freshly squeezed lemon juice. Distribute the preparation into individual bowls, decorate with pieces of the chopped fresh cabe besar and green chilies and serve with warm bread or white rice.

*This dish of Indian origin is a kaleidoscope of aromas and intense flavors that can be difficult to identify at first bite. The pieces of chicken are wrapped in a velvety and tasty cream, and the chilies enhance the delicate chicken meat through the smoothness of the yogurt. A perfect dish for every season, it can be savored with a cup of hot tea or a glass of fresh coconut juice, which among other things, is able to temper the spiciness of the naga morich chili.*

# CHICKEN FILLETS WITH PEANUTS

## INGREDIENTS FOR 4 PEOPLE

1 3/4 LB (800 G) CHICKEN BREAST

2 CLOVES GARLIC

3 TO 4 FRESH DUE MORI CHILI PEPPERS

1 SHALLOT, CHOPPED

1 PINCH GROUND CUMIN

1 PINCH GROUND CORIANDER SEEDS

2 TBSP (30 ML) LIGHT SOY SAUCE

4 TBSP (60 ML) COCONUT MILK

2 TBSP (30 ML) VEGETABLE OIL

7 OZ (200 G) LETTUCE OR SPINACH

SALT

PEPPER

*FOR THE PEANUT SAUCE:*

3 1/2 OZ (100 G) UNSALTED AND SHELLED PEANUTS

6 3/4 FL. OZ (200 ML) COCONUT MILK

2 TBSP (32 G) PEANUT BUTTER

1 TSP (2 G) CURRY

ZEST AND JUICE OF ONE LEMON

1 TSP (2 G) OF SUGAR

3 1/2 FL. OZ (100 ML) OF CREAM

Cut the chicken breasts into thin slices. In a bowl, mix together the freshly peeled and minced garlic cloves, shallots, spices, vegetable oil, soy sauce and coconut milk. Mix well, immerse the chicken, and leave to marinate in the refrigerator for 3 hours. When ready, drain the slices from any excess marinade, and skewer on wooded sticks, curling the pieces so as to give them a wavy shape.

Beforehand, while the chicken is marinating, you should prepare the peanut sauce. First, without any seasoning, roast the dried peanuts in a non-stick pan, then let cool and chop finely. Boil the coconut milk and add the butter and curry powder, stir in the peanuts along with the lemon juice and zest, mixing with care. Then, sweeten the sauce with sugar and drizzle in just enough cream to obtain a smooth mixture. Once the preparation is well blended, put it in the refrigerator until ready to use.

Trim, wash, and dry the salad then keep it wrapped in a damp towel until ready to use. Heat a non-stick pan (or hot plate) and when it is hot cook the skewers for 3-4 minutes on each side; from time to time, brush the meat with the marinade. When they are golden, remove them from the heat, transfer them to a serving dish, laying them on a bed of lettuce and decorate with fresh cut chili. Season with a few tablespoons of marinade and served with the peanut sauce.

*This preparation of Indonesian origin, called chicken 'satay', is perfect for low-calorie diets. In fact, the marinade allows the chicken meat to lighten its already low fat meat and enriches it with a fresh and appetizing taste; also complemented by the chili that can be dosed to taste after cooking so as to not overwhelm all the other flavors. A glass of chilled sparkling white wine is the ideal companion for this fresh and light dish.*

# TANDOORI CHICKEN

Difficulty of preparation: Medium · Degree of difficulty: Medium · Preparation time: 20 minutes · Cooking time: 25-30 minutes · Resting time: 3-5 hours

## INGREDIENTS FOR 4 PEOPLE

1 3/4 LB (800 G) CHICKEN BREAST

6 3/4 FL. OZ (200 ML) PLAIN YOGURT

1 SPRIG CILANTRO

1 OZ (30 G) FRESH GINGER

1 LEMON OR LIME

1/2 TSP POWDERED CAYENNE CHILI PEPPER

1 TBSP GARAM MASALA (SPICE MIXTURE)

1 BEBEBÈ CHILI PEPPER

1/2 TSP (1 G) GROUND TURMERIC

1 TBSP (15 ML) VEGETABLE OIL

SALT

2 DROPS OF RED FOOD COLORING (OPTIONAL)

Cut the chicken breasts in long and rather large pieces and remove any loose fat, skin and bones. Peel and finely chop the garlic, peel and grate the ginger and collect its juice and pulp, then squeeze the lemon. Trim, wash, dry and finely chop the cilantro.

Pour the yogurt into a large container with edges. Stir in the garam masala then add the garlic, cayenne chili, turmeric, chopped cilantro, ginger, salt, coloring (optional), lemon juice and oil. Mix all the ingredients well until the mixture is well blended and without lumps. Immerse the chicken breast in the mixture and let it marinate for at least 3 hours, even potentially up to 5.

Preheat the oven to 390° F (200° C); take the chicken out from the marinade and transfer it in to a baking dish with its marinade, and bake for 25 to 30 minutes. Then, remove it from the oven, place in a dish and cover with its sauce. Decorate with freshly sliced yellow bebebè pepper. Great warm, this chicken can also be served cold, if cut into thin slices.

*The original recipe calls for baking in the* tandoor, *a typical Punjab (Indian) cylindrical clay oven, whose feature is to smoke food as well as cook it, giving the food the aroma and special taste that characterizes them. Tandoori chicken is perhaps the best known Indian recipe and is usually served with chapati bread. Those who wish for a bright red color can add a few drops of food coloring to the marinade. The garam masala, which gives the dish that exotic and extremely tasty aroma, is a mixture of pepper, cinnamon, cardamom, ginger, cumin, garlic, black pepper, cloves, nutmeg. If you want to experiment you can prepare it at home, but is now also found in supermarkets! Cold beer or tea drinks are best suited for this fragrant and spicy dish.*

# PORK CHOPS WITH FRUIT

Difficulty of preparation: Easy - Degree of difficulty: Easy - Preparation time: 15 minutes - Cooking time: 8 minutes

## INGREDIENTS FOR 4 PEOPLE

4 PORK CHOPS

1 SMALL PINEAPPLE

1/2 HEAD OF CURLY LETTUCE

1 FRESH ACROBATA CHILI PEPPER

4 TBSP (60 ML) EXTRA VIRGIN OLIVE OIL

SALT AND BLACK PEPPERCORNS

With a sharp knife, cut the pineapple and slice off the top which you can later use for garnish, along with other pieces of the fruit. Peel the pineapple and divide it lengthwise into quarters and eliminate the central part that is hard and woody. Cut the pulp into chunks and, if you can, collect the juice that is produced during this operation into a bowl.

Trim, wash and drain the curly lettuce then break up the leaves into irregular pieces and let them dry on a kitchen towel. Wash and cut the peppers, place in a bowl, then add the oil, any pineapple juice, then add salt and freshly ground pepper to taste. Put the meat to marinate in this sauce for 5 minutes.

Just before cooking the pork chops, spread the salad on a plate with some pieces of pineapple. Preheat a hot plate, drain the slices of pork from the marinade and cook them a few minutes on each side. Turn them several times until you have a uniform and inviting color then transfer them to a plate. Season the pork chops with some drops of marinade and cover them with pieces of pineapple. Serve immediately in order to appreciate the contrast between the hot meat and the fresh and juicy pineapple.

*Due to its high concentration of bromelain, pineapple is often paired with lamb and pork, because it promotes the digestion of proteins and fats found in meat. Furthermore, it is rich in fiber and is therefore good for general well-being of the body. Due to the high content of vitamin C in the chili, this excellent tasting dish is also a valuable aid in the cold season. For "pineapple" means a fruit that is wide spread and found in many varieties, differing in size, smell and taste, some of which can be very sweet or sour. When purchasing pineapple, remember to make sure it is firm and fragrant with a tuft of dark green and healthy leaves. A light and very cold beer can accompany this fresh and fragrant dish.*

# SPICY RIBS WITH MEAT

## INGREDIENTS FOR 4 PEOPLE

1 3/4 LB (800 G) PORK RIBS
1 ONION
1 GARLIC CLOVE
1 BODYGUARD CHILI PEPPER
1 OZ (30 G) FRESH MINT
2 LIMES
4 TBSP (60 ML) EXTRA VIRGIN OLIVE OIL
SALT

FOR THE SAUCE:
1/2 CUP (115 ML) CIDER VINEGAR
2 TBSP (20 G) CHOPPED ONIONS
3 TBSP (45 G) MUSTARD
3 TBSP (41 G) BROWN SUGAR
2 TBSP (30 ML) KETCHUP
2 CLOVES
1 PINCH OF CAYENNE PEPPER

Trim and wash the mint, then finely chop half of it. Arrange the ribs in a large dish then add salt and sprinkle with the chopped mint. Set aside for 30 minutes. In the meantime, prepare the sauce. Put the vinegar and two tablespoons of chopped onion in a saucepan. Cook on low heat for 5 minutes, then strain out the vinegar, put the onion back in the pan, then add the mustard, sugar, ketchup, cloves and cayenne pepper, mix carefully so that the various ingredients dissolve and blend well. Cook on medium heat until the mixture thickens and caramelizes.

Take the ribs from the pan and brush them one by one with the prepared sauce. Arrange the ribs on a hot barbecue grill and cook until they are well and evenly roasted. While cooking, spread the sauce over them again until there is none left.

Meanwhile, peel the onion and garlic, chop them finely, mix them with the chili pepper and a few mint leaves, transfer them into a bowl, add the oil, lime juice and pieces of line, then add to the ribs and mix so that they are flavored with the dressing. Serve immediately garnished with mint.

*The delicious combination of mint and lime refine the ribs, giving the meat a fresh and light flavor. The hotness of chili harmonizes all the ingredients well, giving the recipe spicy and bright tones in contrast with those of the aromatic herb and citrus; slightly reminiscent of lemon but is less sour. This recipe of Vietnamese origin can be enjoyed right off the grill or at room temperature, along with white rice or a raw vegetable salad. Some aromatic and fragrant green tea would be perfect to go along with the ribs. If you prefer a glass of wine instead, it is best to pick a dry white.*

# PORK LOIN WITH PEPPERS AND LIME

Difficulty of preparation: Easy - Degree of difficulty: Easy - Preparation time: 20 minutes - Cooking time: 10 minutes - Resting time: 30 minutes

## INGREDIENTS FOR 4 PEOPLE

1 LB (500 G) PORK LOIN

3 1/2 OZ (100 G) BEAN SPROUTS

2 CARROTS

2 GREEN BELL PEPPERS

2 RED BELL PEPPERS

3 THAI CHILI PEPPERS

4 CLOVES GARLIC

6 TBSP (90 ML) SWEET SOY SAUCE

2 LIMES

8 TBSP (120 ML) FISH SAUCE

5 FL. OZ (150 ML) BROTH

1 1/2 TSP (3 1/2 G) CORNSTARCH

2 TBSP (30 ML) SOY OIL

1 TSP (2 1/2 G) FRESHLY GROUND WHITE PEPPER

Squeeze one lime, grind the chili peppers, then peel the garlic and chop finely. Prepare a sauce with the lime juice, chilies, garlic, soy and the fish sauces, broth, freshly ground pepper and corn starch. Stir until the mixture is well blended.

Place the meat on a cutting board and with a sharp knife cut it into strips of 1/3-inch wide by 1 1/3-inch long. Transfer the meat to a bowl and add the sauce, stir and leave to marinate for 30 minutes. Trim the bean sprouts, then wash and drain them. Peel the carrots and cut them into 'matchsticks'. Wash the peppers, remove the stems, seeds and white parts then cut into strips.

Pour the oil into a wok. Heat the oil, then add the carrots and peppers and cook for 5 minutes while stirring, then move them to the side of the pan. Drain the meat from the sauce and cook for 2 minutes in the middle of the wok while stirring frequently then move this to the side as well. Finally, pour in the marinade, stir in the other ingredients, add the bean sprouts and continue cooking and stirring for about a minute. Once cooked, remove from heat and serve the dish garnished with freshly cut lime slices.

*This preparation, originally from Thailand, is a mix of expressive flavors, in which you taste both spicy and aromatic notes. It is perfect to enjoy on its own or along with white rice; a food that nicely absorbs the spicy chili. The freshness of the sprouts is almost unchanged after brief cooking, which maintain their delicate and juicy texture. Serve this dish with aromatic black tea or if you prefer a glass of wine then try a lively red with a low alcohol content, which is the most suitable for this dish.*

# TAMALES

## INGREDIENTS FOR 4 PEOPLE

12 OUTER LEAVES OF DRIED CORN (AVAILABLE
   IN SPECIALTY MEXICAN FOOD STORES)
2 DUCK BREASTS
17 1/2 OZ (500 G) CANNED BEANS
1 FRESH RED HABANERO PEPPER
1 CHEIRO CHILI PEPPER
2 CLOVES GARLIC
1 ONION

1 PINCH GROUND CUMIN
2 TOMATOES
1 RED BELL PEPPER
2 TBSP (30 ML) OLIVE OIL
TABASCO SAUCE
SALT
FRESHLY GROUND PEPPER

Soak the corn leaves in hot water for 2 hours. Wash the beans and rinse away the canned water, then let drip drain in a colander. Wash the chili peppers, remove their stems, white parts and seeds then chop. Peel the garlic and liquefy with half of the beans and chili in a blender. Season with pepper, cumin and salt to taste. Blanch the tomatoes in order to peel the skin off easily then remove the seeds and dice into cubes. Wash the bell pepper, remove its stems, white parts and seeds then chop. Peel the onion and cut into small pieces.

Singe the duck breasts over a high flame to remove any small feathers then cut the fillets into thin slices, just under a quarter-inch thick and brown in hot oil. Salt and pepper the duck to taste. Interrupt cooking after about 2 minutes. In the same pan, brown the chopped onion, add the tomatoes and cook everything for 2 to 3 minutes, then add the bell pepper and half the whole beans, add salt and flavor with Tabasco. Continue cooking for 5 minutes, then remove from heat.

In the meantime, drain the corn leaves, spread them on a kitchen towel, dry them well and fill them with a tablespoon of mashed beans. Then distribute the meat and vegetable mixture on top. Roll the leaves lengthwise, fold the ends and tie to close with kitchen string. Cook the tamales in a steamer for 30 minutes. Once cooked, distribute them on a platter and serve hot.

*This is a beautiful dish, both very fragrant and very spicy. The color of the tamale wrap can vary from beige, if you use the dried leaves as explained here, to light green, in case you manage to find fresh leaves instead. In any case, they give the preparation a slight scent of grass that fits beautifully with the other ingredients. A dark beer with a high alcohol percentage is the ideal drink to go with tamales.*

# MAGHREBI STYLE LAMB

*Difficulty of preparation: medium-difficult - Degree of difficulty: medium-difficult - Preparation time: 20 minutes - Cooking time: 3 hours*

## INGREDIENTS FOR 4 PEOPLE

2 1/5 LB (1 KG) LAMB SHOULDER

1 1/3 LB (600 G) ONIONS

1 TBSP (6 G) CUMIN SEEDS

1 TSP (2 G) POWDERED GINGER

1 TSP (2 G) CORIANDER SEEDS

1/2 TSP (1 G) DRIED ACI SIVRI CHILI PEPPER

1 TBSP (2 G) SAFFRON

2 CLOVES GARLIC

2 CANDIED LEMONS

1 LEMON

3 1/2 OZ (100 G) BLACK OLIVES

6 TBSP (90 ML) OLIVE OIL

SALT

Peel the onions and garlic. Cut the onions and finely chop the garlic. Cut the lamb shoulder into pieces. Mix all the spices together, squeeze the juice out of lemon and chop the candied fruit into four parts.

In a saucepan with high sides, pour in four tablespoons of olive oil, brown the meat, add the candied fruit and sprinkle with the lemon juice. Stir and cook on high heat for 5 minutes, frequently moving the pieces so that they mix well with the other ingredients. Then, reduce to low heat, add the spices, the chopped chili pepper and 1 clove of garlic, cover and let simmer for 3 hours. While this is cooking, salt to taste and stir from time to time.

About 30 minutes before the end, pour the equivalent of two tablespoons of olive oil in a pan and sauté the onions and 1 clove of garlic. Cook over low heat just up until the onions become soft and almost brittle then transfer them into the stew, add the olives, stir well and turn off the stove. When serving, arrange the lamb stew on a platter and serve this tasty, aromatic and spicy dish with boiled potatoes or white rice.

*The North African, or Tajine, lamb is a stewed meat from the traditional earthenware pot called Tajine, completely made of terracotta and composed of two parts: a flat base to lay the dishes on and a tapered conic portion to overlap, whose shape allows the recovery of the condensation that forms while cooking, so that you get food that is always soft and tender. The Tajine was once placed directly over the coals for very slow and soft roasting. You can prepare the lamb stew in steel pots, provided that they have a thick bottom and the ability to cook less aggressively. Hot mint tea is an excellent beverage to accompany this dish. If you prefer wine, chose among the full-bodied reds with robust and deep flavors.*

# ISCHIAN RABBIT

## INGREDIENTS FOR 4 PEOPLE

1 RABBIT, CLEANED (ABOUT 2 TO 2 1/4 LB / 1 KG)

14 OZ (400 G) CHERRY TOMATOES

2 GARLIC CLOVES

1 SALAMANDRA CHILI PEPPER

1 BUNCH BASIL

1 BUNCH THYME

1 BUNCH MARJORAM

1 BUNCH ROSEMARY

1 SPRIG SAGE

1/2 CUP (115 ML) DRY WHITE WINE

OLIVE OIL

RED WINE VINEGAR

SALT

Cut the rabbit into pieces and wash under cold running water. Remove any fatty parts. To eliminate the gamey flavor that sometimes remains in the flesh, immerse the pieces in cold water with two tablespoons of vinegar per liter and let stand for 10 minutes, then drain through a colander and pat dry with a kitchen towel. Meanwhile, peel the tomatoes, then take half of them and make a small cut in each, while leaving the other ones whole. Trim all the herbs, remove the hard and woody parts, and finely chop half of them.

Heat the equivalent of six tablespoons of oil in a large non-stick frying pan and sauté the garlic and chili whole. When you smell the inviting scent of garlic, add the meat and brown over high heat until the pieces are evenly golden. At this point add the wine, let the alcohol evaporate, reduce the heat, spread on the chopped herbs, stir, add salt to taste and cover. Cook over low heat for 5 minutes, making sure that it doesn't burn.

Finally, add the washed cherry tomatoes to the pan, lightly squeezing those that have been cut. Then continue cooking for 30 to 35 minutes, turning the pieces several times and making sure the bottom does not dry out too much; if that is the case you can add warm water. Once cooked, remove from heat, transfer the rabbit to a dish, season with herbs and serve hot.

*This traditional country dish, from Ischia to be exact, sums up the typical characteristics of an intriguing island, cheerful and sunny as only the land of the south can be. Its strong and delicious colors wrap the tender and light white meat of the rabbit. Tantalizing aromas announce this exquisite dish with sweet tones; a dish that is easy to create and tempting to enjoy! Red wines are the right company for the Ischian rabbit.*

# THAI STYLE SURF
# AND TURF FONDUE

Difficulty of preparation: Medium - Degree of difficulty: Medium - Preparation time: 1 hour - Cooking time: 70 minutes - Resting time: 35 minutes

## INGREDIENTS FOR 4 PEOPLE

10 OZ (300 G) WHITE-FLESHED
   FISH FILLETS

14 OZ (400 G) CHICKEN BREAST

4 CUPS (1 L) CHICKEN BROTH

12 RAW SHRIMP

1 WHITE ONION

3 CLOVES GARLIC

1 OZ (30 G) FRESH GINGER

3 THAI CHILI PEPPERS

2 LEMONGRASS STEMS

10 OZ (300 G) FRESH SPINACH

1 3/4 OZ (50 G) RICE NOODLES

1 TSP (2 G) POTATO STARCH

ZEST AND JUICE OF 1 LEMON

4 TBSP (60 ML) FISH SAUCE

4 SPRIGS CILANTRO

SALT

Wash the shrimp and remove the shell, leaving the tail; cut the chicken into cubes and
dredge them in the potato starch; wash and the fish then cut into small pieces. Store these
ingredients in the fridge until ready to use.

Peel the garlic and onion, then chop coarsely. Peel the ginger and cut into thin slices. Trim and
wash the peppers then cut into rings. Wash the lemongrass and break up into fairly big pieces.
Pour the broth into a pot, add all these ingredients that have just been prepared and simmer for
1 hour on low heat. Trim the spinach and leave to soak for 30 minutes in cold water, then rinse
several times, drain and keep in a damp towel until ready to use. When the broth is ready, add
the lemon juice and zest, turn off the stove and let it rest for 5 minutes then strain and pour the
broth into the fondue container and add the fish sauce. Keep the broth warm with a lit flame.
Wash the cilantro, break it up into pieces and add to the broth.

Separately, boil the rice noodles in salted water for 3 minutes, then drain, pass under cold water
and leave to dry. Divide the chicken, shrimp, fish and spinach into individual containers and bring
the hot broth to the table. Using fondue cutlery or wooden sticks, each diner can cook the
various ingredients themselves. Finally, in single portion bowls, pour in a ladle full of broth
and immerse the rice noodles: the soup will conclude the course.

*This recipe of Thai origin is a mix of delicate flavors that are reinforced by the chili peppers. The
herbs make the soup very fresh and fragrant, in which it is wonderful to taste the various meats,
immersed for a few moments for light and barely visible cooking. A bold and fruity white wine
is ideal for this dish.*

# SPICY PRAWNS WITH ORANGE AND THYME

Difficulty of preparation: Easy - Degree of difficulty: Easy - Preparation time: 10 minutes - Cooking time: 5-10 minutes - Resting time: 1 hour

## INGREDIENTS FOR 4 PEOPLE

2 TO 2 1/4 LB (1 KG) FRESH
   PRAWNS
1 CLOVE GARLIC
10 SPRIGS OF THYME

1 ORGANIC ORANGE
1 DRIED SUAVITO CHILI PEPPER
2 TBSP (30 ML) EXTRA VIRGIN OLIVE OIL
SALT

Crush the dried chili in a mortar. Trim and wash the thyme, dry (blot with paper towels) and break up coarsely. Wash the orange and zest the peel. Juice the orange and set the zest aside.

Peel and chop the garlic. Mix together the orange juice and zest, the garlic, half of the thyme, two tablespoons of extra virgin olive oil, salt to taste and plenty of chili pepper. Rinse the shrimp under cold running water, then drain well and place in a bowl. Pour the orange marinade over them, stir and leave in the refrigerator for 1 hour, mixing several times so that the sauce is absorbed by shellfish.

Preheat the oven to 390° F (200° C), place the prawns on a baking sheet covered with wax paper, pour a few tablespoons of marinade on top and bake for 5 minutes. The cooking time is at your own discretion. There are those who love seafood barely cooked so that it can retain its natural freshness, while others prefer a longer cooking time: if this is the case with you, let them cook for another 3 to 5 minutes. When cooked, remove the pan from the oven then place the prawns onto a platter and garnish with thyme and a few drops of marinade. Serve the dish with slices of toasted rustic bread.

*This dish can be made with a less spicy chili, so as not to overpower the delicate flavor of the shrimp or with a much stronger variety in order to develop – along with the orange, garlic and thyme – a wonderful balance of flavors and fragrances. It is a rich second course dish with a refined and elegant taste, perfect in any season. A glass of chilled white wine, both aromatic and fragrant, is the ideal drink to emphasize the harmony of the shrimp with orange.*

# SHRIMPS WITH HABANERO MOUSSE

## INGREDIENTS FOR 4 PEOPLE

16 FRESH SHRIMP

2 CLOVES GARLIC

2 TBSP (30 ML) TOMATO SAUCE

1 TBSP (30 ML) SOY SAUCE

1 TBSP (30 ML) HABANERO MOUSSE

  OR 1 RED HABANERO PEPPER

EXTRA VIRGIN OLIVE OIL

SALT

If you don't have the habanero mousse, you can prepare it at home: wash the habanero, remove the stems and seeds, in a blender, liquefy the chili with a drizzle of oil until the pepper absorbs it. When you get a smooth paste, transfer the mixture into a container, or divide it into small beads and keep in the freezer this way. Peel the garlic and chop finely.

Thoroughly wash the shrimp in cold running water. In a pan, pour two tablespoons of olive oil, sauté the garlic, add the shrimp and soy sauce, and after a minute, add the tomato sauce and chili mousse then mix all the ingredients.

Lave the pan on high heat for 2 to 3 minutes, stirring so as to get a homogeneous mixture. Add salt to taste and serve the prawns piping hot, accompanied with toasted bread or white rice.

*This is a quick dish to prepare and very tasty for true lovers of strong chili. In fact, the habanero is one of the hottest varieties in the world, but at the same time has a great and very aromatic taste. In addition to making very spicy dishes, it can also flavor them immensely, which is an experience that is worth trying even for those less accustomed to chili. Soft white bread is perfect to accompany this second course dish, because it is able to absorb the spiciness. It is a perfect recipe for the summer, because it seems that the chili can promote the lowering of body temperature! A nice mug of cold beer, in addition to being the best drink to enjoy with the shrimp and habanero mousse, is also able to reduce the fiery feeling that can be perceived at first bite.*

# PRAWNS WITH YOGURT AND CHILI

Difficulty of preparation: Easy - Degree of difficulty: Easy - Preparation time: 5 minutes - Cooking time: 40-50 second - Resting time: 1 hour

## INGREDIENTS FOR 4 PEOPLE

1 1/3 LB (600 G) FRESH PRAWNS

7 OZ (200 G) CREAMY NATURAL YOGURT

1 CLOVE GARLIC

2 DRIED BESLER'S CHERRY PEPPERS

5 SPRIGS OF MINT

1 TBSP (15 ML) EXTRA VIRGIN OLIVE OIL

1 TBSP (15 ML) LEMON JUICE

SALT

Squeeze the juice out of the lemon, strain it and keep aside until ready to use. Trim the mint, wash and dry it and break up half into small pieces. Peel and finely chop the garlic, clean the chilies with a damp cloth and crush them in a mortar. Mix the yogurt with the garlic clove, the chopped mint, one tablespoon of extra virgin olive oil, the lemon juice and the hot pepper that you can dose at will. Let the sauce rest in the refrigerator for at least 1 hour.

Gently wash the pink shrimp under running water, then bring a pot of salted water to a boil and throw in the shellfish for a few seconds, about 30-40 (shrimp is a very delicate meat, therefore let them cook just long enough to make them lose their transparency). Then drain them, pass them under cold water to stop them from cooking and remove the shells.

Put the shrimp in individual bowls, divide the sauce and distribute it onto the shellfish. Decorate each serving with a few leaves of mint. If you prefer, you can serve the sauce in separate bowls, so that the diners can season to their own taste.

*Refined, beautiful and tasty, this is a great second course dish, very light and very easy to prepare. The only risk is cooking the shrimp, which should be able to retain their natural freshness, in order not to lose the water that they are enriched with. These shrimp are great steamed or slightly blanched, but do not be afraid to leave them on the stove a little while. However, the more you cook them, the tougher and more tasteless they become. The combination of yogurt with chili pepper is a wonderful contrast between the various flavors of this dish, and if you reduce the doses it can be transformed into an entrée. A light and fresh white wine, such as prosecco (sparkling wine) or champagne would be the ideal drink to best appreciate this delicious dish.*

# LOBSTER IN SPICY SAUCE

## INGREDIENTS FOR 4 PEOPLE

2 LOBSTERS, APPROXIMATELY 2 TO 2 1/4 LB (1 KG) EACH

1 RED TROPEA ONION

1 GLASS DRY WHITE WINE

2 POWDERED DADDY CHILIES

3 TBSP (45 ML) EXTRA VIRGIN OLIVE OIL

SALT

*FOR THE COURT-BOUILLON:*

1 ONION

1 CARROT

2 SPRIGS PARSLEY

2 SPRIGS WILD FENNEL

Wash and peel the vegetables for the court-bouillon and slice them. Trim the herbs. Put the vegetables and the herbs in lot of salted water then bring to a boil. Meanwhile, pass the lobster under running water and immerse into the pot. Cook for 8 to 10 minutes, then drain and allow to cool for 5 minutes on a cutting board. Remove the heads of the lobsters and, with scissors, open the shells along the abdomen, remove the flesh and cut into slices of between 1/3 and 1/2 inch thick.

Filter the cooking broth and keep it warm until ready to use. Peel the onion and slice finely. Grind the chilies in a mortar. Dissolve the saffron in the hot broth. Pour the olive oil into a non-stick pan, soften the onions and after about 2 minutes add the wine. Let the wine evaporate and pour in the broth with the dissolved saffron. Simmer to reduce by half, stirring constantly, then add the lobster slices and turn off the stove. Add salt, sprinkle with plenty of ground chili and drizzle with the cooking sauce.

When ready to serve, place a base of yellow onions on a platter and place the slices of lobster on top. To the center of the plate, add the head and the shell as a decoration. Serve hot.

*It is a very suitable second course for an exceptional occasion, such as a special anniversary or an important date. First of all due to the effect that the dish creates, thanks to its beauty at the time that it is brought to the table, and then for the elegance of flavors and appetizing contrasts that characterize it. Lobster is a crustacean with a delicate flavor, slightly sweet with a soft texture and the combination with the pepper creates a special spiciness, which makes the dish very appetizing. A pink champagne or prosecco riserva would be the most suitable wines to go with this wonderful dish.*

# COD WITH TOMATOES, OLIVES AND CHILI

## INGREDIENTS FOR 4 PEOPLE

1 3/4 LB (800 G) FRESH COD FILLETS

1 LB (500 G) CHERRY TOMATOES

7 OZ (200 G) SEEDLESS BLACK OLIVES

5 TBSP + 1 TSP (20 G) PARSLEY

2 ONIONS

2 CLOVES GARLIC

1 DRIED AMIGA CHILI PEPPER

2 TBSP (30 ML) OLIVE OIL

SALT

Wash the cod fillets and dry by patting with paper towels. Remove any bones and the skin then arrange them in a steamer, cover and steam (or by placing the steamer basket in a pot with 5 inches of water at the bottom) for about 5 minutes. When cooked, drain the fillets and keep warm and aside.

Trim the parsley, wash it, remove the hard parts and keep the leaves in tufts. Coat a pan with two tablespoons of olive oil, wash the tomatoes and glaze two-thirds of them for about 5 minutes, stirring gently so that they are evenly coated. Add salt, then remove from heat and keep the tomatoes aside and covered until ready to use. Chop the olives into pieces, peel the onion and cut it "brunoise" style (finely diced), then peel the garlic and chop finely. Wash the pepper, dry it and crush it in a mortar. Remove the glazed tomatoes from pan and cut with a sharp knife. Pour the olives, chili pepper, onion and garlic in the same pan and cook on high heat for 2 minutes, then add the last third of the tomatoes and salt to taste.

When serving, arrange the cod fillets in individual dishes and spread a spoonful of the vegetable mix over them. Garnish with fresh parsley and decorate the plates with some raw tomatoes in small clusters; serve immediately.

*This is a fresh and light second course, beautiful to look at and great tasting. The recipe, whose essential difficulty is the need to find the freshest ingredients, is highly digestible and ideal for the warm months. The delicate white flesh of the cod goes well with the spiciness of the chili. The best beverage with which to appreciate this dish is a sauvignon with a magnificent pale yellow color and intoxicating fragrance.*

# SPICY FRITTERS

## INGREDIENTS FOR 4 PEOPLE

| | |
|---|---|
| 14 OZ (400 G) COD FILLETS | 1 ALI CHILI PEPPER |
| 1 BUNCH CHIVES | 1 EGG |
| 1 OZ (30 G) FRESH GINGER | 1 TBSP (15 ML) FISH SAUCE |
| 4 SPRIGS CILANTRO | 1 2/3 CUP (200 G) FLOUR |
| 1 LEMON | 1 1/4 CUP (300 ML) PEANUT OIL |
| 1 ONION | SALT |

Peel the onion and chop finely. Peel and grate the ginger, and collect the pulp. Wash the pepper, remove the stem, seeds and white parts then cut it into very small pieces. Trim, wash and finely chop the chives (keep 5 or 6 stalks for garnish) and the cilantro. Remove any bones and the skin from the cod fillets then cut into pieces to ease with cooking and make the flesh tastier. In a pan, pour two tablespoons of olive oil, sauté the onion, ginger and chili pepper, then cook the cod for 5 minutes on low heat, stirring the pieces frequently so that the flavors are well absorbed. Add salt to taste, turn off the stove and let cool. Mince the fish, add the herbs and put everything in a bowl.

Separately, beat the egg with the fish sauce, add it to the mixture, mix well with wet hands and make flat meatballs. Then cover them in the flour so that they stick well.

In a large pan, heat the oil to approximately 350° F (180° C), on a high and well-spread flame. Dip the fritters in the oil, cook for 2 minutes before you turn them and remove them when they are lightly browned. Serve hot with freshly cut lemon slices and garnished with chives.

*The cod fish, with its fresh and delicate meat, blends perfectly with the chili, which can give it an aromatic and very appetizing character. The fritters are a delicious second course dish to be served with colorful salads made raw vegetables. A glass of chilled dry white wine is the ideal companion.*

# SPICY SALMON

Difficulty of preparation: Easy - Degree of difficulty: Easy - Preparation time: 10 minutes - Cooking time: 15 minutes

INGREDIENTS FOR 4 PEOPLE

1 1/3 LB (600 G) FRESH SALMON FILLETS
2 PICKLED JALAPEÑO PEPPERS
1 RED BELL PEPPER
1 YELLOW BELL PEPPER
2 TBSP (15 G) FLOUR
THYME
4 TBSP (60 ML) EXTRA VIRGIN OLIVE OIL
SALT

Wash the peppers, remove the stems, seeds and white parts then cut into irregular pieces. Drain the jalapeno peppers from the liquid and slice. Trim, wash and dry the thyme then break up irregularly. Clean and skin the salmon, remove any bones, then cut into pieces and slightly flour them.

Pour the oil into a large non-stick pan. Once hot, add the bell peppers. Simmer on low heat for 10 minutes covered with the lid. Then uncover the pan, raise the heat and put the salmon and chili peppers to cook, stirring frequently, on high heat for about 5 minutes, or until the fish cubes are lightly browned. While cooking, add salt to taste and flavor with half the thyme from the recipe.

Remove from heat, transfer the salmon in individual dishes and decorate with the remaining thyme. Serve hot or at room temperature.

*The pieces of salmon with spicy peppers are another very fragrant and colorful dish, which whets the appetite in all senses! The delicate flesh of the fish is filled with the exuberant force of the jalapeño and the peppers worthily accompany the dish with all the freshness and fullness of their pulp. A very balanced dish that brings the joyous and warm tones of summer to the table and in which the delicate taste of the salmon is enhanced by combining it with the hot peppers. A fresh rosé with a low alcohol content would adequately emphasize the lightness of the dish.*

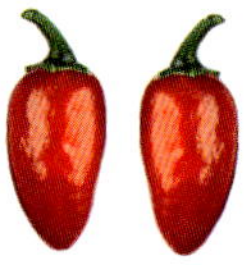

# SEA BASS BAKED IN FOIL WITH POMEGRANATE AND YELLOW AGATA PEPPERS

## INGREDIENTS FOR 4 PEOPLE

2 BASS, ABOUT 1 1/3 LB (600 G) EACH

1 POMEGRANATE

4 FRESH AGATA CHILI PEPPERS

3 1/3 FL. OZ. (100 ML) DRY WHITE WINE

2 STALKS WILD FENNEL

EXTRA VIRGIN OLIVE OIL

SALT

Wash the pomegranate and open it in two, then gently take out the seeds, making sure to remove the white skin, which is quite bitter, then set the seeds aside in a bowl. Wipe the skin of the peppers with a damp cloth and, after removing the stem and seeds, cut into small pieces.

Preheat the oven to 390° F (200° C). Wash the fennel and break it up roughly with your hands. Gut the fish, remove the scales, wash and pat dry with paper towels. Arrange them individually on a piece of waxed paper, season with the herb, chili pepper, pomegranate, wine, salt to taste and a few drops of oil. Close up the waxed paper into wraps, place in a baking dish, and bake for about 30 minutes.

When cooked, turn off the oven, remove the baking dish, transfer the wraps to a platter and serve immediately. Accompany the fish with a green salad.

*The bass is a light fish with a balanced flavor. The association with the sweetness of pomegranate and spicy chili transforms this recipe, of Mediterranean cuisine, into a unique variation of the classic baked fish. Nutritious and suitable for low-calorie diets, this dish has an inviting taste nonetheless. The aromas that emanate from the freshly opened wraps make it an excellent second course dish. It is perfect for good health thanks to the pomegranate seeds that aid digestion and are slightly diuretic, the antioxidant chili pepper, and the bass which is low in fat and rich in minerals. A bold and aromatic white wine is always the most suitable drink for fish, but there is a new trend now that suggests pairing it with a fresh and light red that blends well with the delicacy of white meat.*

# TUNA AND ORANGE SALAD

Difficulty of preparation: Medium - Degree of difficulty: Easy - Preparation time: 30 minutes - Cooking time: 10 minutes

## INGREDIENTS FOR 4 PEOPLE

14 OZ (400 G) FRESH TUNA IN SLICES

2 ORGANIC ORANGES

4 SPRIGS THYME

EXTRA VIRGIN OLIVE OIL

1 DOLCEVITA CHILI PEPPER

1 IDEALINO CHILI PEPPER

SALT

Trim the thyme and break it up irregularly. Wash and dry the oranges, peel only one of the two fruits, remove the white parts and then cut the peel into matchsticks. Clean the orange wedges of the skin that surrounds them, making sure to do this gently to avoid damaging the pieces. Cut the other orange in half, squeeze out the juice, strain and pour it into a bowl, add salt, two tablespoons of olive oil and freshly chopped chilies.

Whisk the ingredients well to mix the flavors together and set aside until ready to use. Preheat the oven to 350° F (180° C). Grease a baking dish with a layer of oil, arrange the slices of tuna, bake them in the oven for 10 minutes, then remove the pan and let cool.

When ready to serve, arrange the slices on a plate, alternating with orange and tuna slices, season with the dressing and decorate with the citrus peel and a few sprigs of thyme.

*Here we have a dish with a wonderful contrast of flavors given by the acidity of the orange, the tastiness of the tuna and the spicy aroma of the chilies. Pleasant, appetizing, light and digestible, it is a fast dish to prepare that could originate from southern Italy, where tuna fishing allows an abundance of this significant tasty meat, particularly fat but full of useful nutrients, such as vitamins and minerals. You can adjust the dose of chili to your taste, either increasing the aromatic spiciness or vice versa. Freshly squeezed orange juice or warm aromatic tea are both perfect for this dish. If you want to accompany it with a glass of wine, it's best to opt for a full-bodied and slightly acidic red.*

# SPICY OCTOPUS IN RED AND YELLOW

## INGREDIENTS FOR 4 PEOPLE

2 TO 2 1/4 LB (1 KG) SMALL OCTOPUS

1 LB PEELED TOMATOES

1 SMALL ONION

2 CELERY STALKS

4 DRIED CAPEZZOLI DI SCIMMIA CHILI PEPPERS

1/5 TSP (0.15 G) SAFFRON

3 1/3 FL. OZ. (100 ML) VEGETABLE BROTH

8 SLICES OF BREAD, HOME-MADE IF AVAILABLE

SALT

Remove the intestines, eyes and beak from the octopuses, then rinse well and place in a pot with enough water to cover them. Cook for 5 minutes, then drain, skin and cut into pieces. Heat the broth and keep it warm until ready to use. Crush the chilies in a mortar, after having removed the stem and seeds.

Crush the tomatoes with a fork, peel the onion and slice it, wash and chop the celery. Dissolve the saffron in the hot broth. In a pan, pour two tablespoons of olive oil and sauté the onion and celery, then add the tomatoes and cook on medium heat until the sauce is reduced by half. At that point, add the saffron, chili and small pieces of octopus.

Continue cooking for about 10 minutes on medium-low heat, then try the texture of the octopus meat: if it is to your liking, turn off the stove, if not, let it cook longer. Serve the hot and spicy octopus immediately and serve with slices of homemade bread.

*Its beautiful colors make this dish extraordinary and very tasty. Furthermore, the aroma is very inviting and the fragrance of bread complements this delicious and tasty preparation. There are two schools of thought on how we should cook octopus in order to appreciate it best: according to one it should be cooked very little, and yet the other one favors longer cooking that leads to a softer texture. This recipe can be prepared following the method that reassures you the most and that you know better: the taste for either crunchy or soft, in particular, is a very personal choice! Also, with regards to the tolerance of hot peppers, it is worth trying to adjust the amount so as to achieve what is perfect for your own palate. To accompany this dish we recommend a dry white wine that captures the scents of the Mediterranean and sea salt.*

# CURLY CALAMARI WITH PEPPERS

## INGREDIENTS FOR 4 PEOPLE

1 LB (500 G) CALAMARI

1 ONION

1 CLOVE GARLIC, MINCED

1 RED BELL PEPPER

1 YELLOW BELL PEPPER

4 CONQUISTADOR CHILI PEPPERS

2 TBSP (30 ML) FISH SAUCE

1 TBSP (15 ML) RICE VINEGAR

2 TBSP (25 G) CANE SUGAR

1 TBSP (8 G) CORNSTARCH

3 TBSP (45 ML) SOYBEAN OIL

SALT

Wash and skin the calamari, separate the bag from the tentacles and remove the entrails; cut the flesh into squares of 3 to 4 inches and with a sharp knife make parallel diagonal cross cuts to each piece. Doing this will help the squid to curl when they cook, taking the form of small pine cones.

Trim the bell peppers, remove the stem, seeds and white parts then cut into small pieces. Proceed in the same way with the chili peppers. Peel the onion and slice thinly, heat the oil in a frying pan, and brown the onion, then add the garlic and chili pepper, stir and leave on low heat for 2 minutes, then add the bell peppers and continue to cook for another 5 minutes.

Add salt to taste, stir regularly and at the end add the calamari. Continue cooking over low heat for another 5 minutes. In a bowl, mix the fish sauce, vinegar, sugar and two tablespoons of water. Dissolve the cornstarch into the sauce, stirring everything together until the mixture is smooth and without lumps. Then pour it into the pan with the other ingredients, stir and as soon as the sauce thickens remove from heat. Distribute the squid with peppers into individual dishes and serve immediately, while it is still hot.

*This dish of Thai origin, which is very nice to look at and very fragrant, will enchant you with its sweet and sour flavor. It is a very quick and easy dish to prepare, but greatly satisfying to the palate. The cuts that are made into the squid allow the sauce to absorb into the depths of the meat. Cooking also benefits the final result, giving the mollusk a particular softness. Hot sake is a good drink with which to enjoy this light second course dish made of squid and peppers.*

# SCALLOPS WITH MASHED BEANS AND CHILI

Difficulty of preparation: Easy - Degree of difficulty: Medium - Preparation time: 20 minutes - Cooking time: 15-18 minutes - Resting time: 5 minutes

## INGREDIENTS FOR 4 PEOPLE

12 SCALLOPS IN THEIR SHELLS

3 TBSP (32 G) SALTED BLACK BEANS

1 OZ (30 G) FRESH GINGER

1 DRIED BASSOTTO CHILI PEPPER

1 CLOVE GARLIC

1 TSP (2 G) SICHUAN PEPPER

1 GREEN ONION

2 TBSP (30 ML) LIGHT SOY SAUCE

1 TBSP (15 ML) DRY SHERRY WINE

2 TBSP (30 ML) CHICKEN BROTH

4 TBSP (60 ML) OLIVE OIL

1 TBSP (15 ML) SESAME SEED OIL

1 TSP (3 G) SESAME SEEDS

Soak the beans in warm water for 5 minutes, then rinse, drain and mash with the prongs of a fork until you get an irregular puree. Clean up the scallops thoroughly by passing them under cold running water. Open them with a sharp knife and remove the flat side of the shell.

Leave the scallops in the concave part of their shell and place them in a basket for steaming. Close the steamer and cook for about 9 minutes, then remove them and let them cool in the air. Peel the onion and set aside some of the green parts for garnish. Peel the garlic, then chop finely. Crush the chili in a mortar. Peel the ginger and chop it, collecting the juice and pulp. Prepare the sauce which will be used to flavor the mussels by pouring the olive oil, garlic, chili, ginger and blacks beans in a pan and cook on low heat, blending it all together for a minute. At this point, turn up the heat and add the soy sauce, sherry and broth. Continue cooking for 5 minutes, stirring constantly, and finally add the sesame seed oil and the Sichuan pepper.

When ready to serve, transfer the scallops to a serving plate and spread the sauce over them. Garnish the dish with slices of chili pepper, chopped green onion and sesame seeds.

*This second course dish is simple enough but should be followed very closely when preparing the sauce, which must be very hot when the sherry is poured in so as to blend well and begin to boil immediately; this will prevent the sauce from acquiring a slightly bitter taste. Adjust even doses of soy sauce according to your taste, in such a way that its savory flavor does not dominate the other ingredients. Accompany the scallops with a glass of white wine.*

# SPICY ANCHOVIES WITH FENNEL

## INGREDIENTS FOR 4 PEOPLE

2 TO 2 1/4 LB (1 KG) FRESH ANCHOVIES

3 TBSP + 1 TSP (20 G) WILD FENNEL

2 CLOVES GARLIC

1 DRIED ABBRACCIO CHILI PEPPER

1/2 CUP (100 ML) DRY WHITE WINE

EXTRA VIRGIN OLIVE OIL

SALT

Wash the anchovies, gut them gently, remove the head and the central spine, pass them one by one under running water, then pat them dry with paper towels and lay them flat spread out like an open book onto a plate.

Wash and dry the fennel, then chop finely. Peel and crush the garlic. Pour the equivalent of two tablespoons of oil in a frying pan and fry the garlic and freshly crumbled chili. When the garlic begins to spread a beautiful and appetizing aroma in the kitchen, remove from the pan and put the anchovies in the hot oil to cook. Bath with the wine and cook for about 5 minutes, stirring gently to avoid damaging the fish. Add salt to taste.

While cooking, season the dish with half of the fennel and adjust the flame so that the wine evaporates at the same time that the fish is cooked. When finished, transfer the anchovy fillets to a platter, decorate with the remaining fennel and serve immediately.

*Anchovies with wild fennel is a traditional Sardinian seafood dish. The wild fennel offers a particularly enticing aroma that brings the few other ingredients into perfect harmony, and our addition of chili peppers gives this version a spicy touch. The recipe is quite simple. Although it can be difficult to clean the anchovies, you can bypass the issue by buying them already cleaned. Also, be sure to use a pan that's large enough to cook the fish in a single layer with no overlapping. The best wine to use in this recipe – and to enjoy with the finished dish at the table! – would be crisp and fragrant, with mineral and citrus notes. Ask your local to direct you to a Vermentino, and serve well chilled.*

# SPICY FISH FILLETS

## INGREDIENTS FOR 4 PEOPLE

4 SLICES OF COD

1 LEMON

1 LIME

2 TBSP (30 ML) MELTED GHEE
  (CLARIFIED BUTTER)

1 INDIANO CHILI PEPPER

1 STALK LEMONGRASS

SALT

*FOR THE MARINADE:*

13 1/2 OZ (400 G) YOGURT

1 ONION

3 TBSP (45 ML) VINEGAR

5 GARLIC CLOVES

1 OZ (30 G) GINGER

1 TSP (2 G) POWDERED TURMERIC

1 TSP (2 G) GROUND CORIANDER

1 TSP (2 G) GARAM MASALA (SPICE MIXTURE)

1 GROUND FATALII CHILI PEPPER

1 TSP (2 G) FRESHLY GROUND PEPPER

SALT

Peel and grate the ginger, collecting both the juice and pulp. Peel the garlic and chop finely. Wash the lemon grass and keep it aside until ready to use. Squeeze the lemon and the lime, and pour the juice into a bowl. Eliminate any bones from the fish and put the cod slices in the juice. Add salt to taste. Grease a mold (those used for plum cake) with ghee – the clarified butter used in Indian cooking – and arrange the slices of cod.

Mix all the ingredients for the marinade in a container with two tablespoons of water and pour the sauce resulting sauce over the fish. Then let it rest covered in the refrigerator for 2 hours, stirring from time to time. Preheat oven to 350° F (180° C) and bake the fish with the marinade inside the mold. Cook for 30 minutes. When finished, transfer the cod fillets into four individual bowls and season with plenty of sauce.

Wash the chili peppers, cut into rings directly onto the plates and do the same with the lemongrass. Serve the fish while it is still warm, and accompany with crusty bread, bread sticks or white rice.

*This Indian-inspired second course dish mixes aromas and colors that are unusual in the rest of the world, but in the country of origin, it creates a spontaneous harmony that is hard for us to imagine. When thinking about these ingredients combined with each other, in fact, it is difficult to predict what flavor the dish will have once everything is together. The recipe must be tried in order to appreciate its complex and the particular balance. The use of the oven allows even baking, in which it 'collects' the aromas and makes them emerge cheerfully in a real victory only at the end of cooking once you open the oven to take out the mold. Furthermore, the choice of an enveloping container causes the meat to be well surrounded by the seasoning and to soak up the spices and flavorings. Hot green tea or a cold glass of dry wine would be the perfect companion for this dish of spicy cod.*

# SIDE DISHES

What would a main course of meat or fish (or even a bowl of rice) be without the side dish? A picture without a frame, a final draft without the dotted I's and crossed T's. Side dishes are sometimes so good they can compete with the main course for the starring role in your meal. Such is the case of the tasty stuffed green peppers, rich in the flavor and aroma of the typical Mexican fatalii, which even in a secondary role, can be a perfect fit for just about any dish.

Side dishes are not only delicious, they are also useful for our well-being: they can deliver lots of vitamins and minerals, fiber and carbohydrates with every forkful of herbs or spoonful of lentils. This, of course, is also a part of cooking, turning the food we need for our health into tasty, delicious recipes. After all, an unappetizing dish can be very difficult to eat!

In the peasant kitchens of long ago, especially those of rural Italy, where food was once scarce and variety was difficult to come by, we find the origins of many recipes that transform greens, turnips, cauliflower and other humble vegetables into simple, yet extremely inviting dishes. Combined with spices, perfumes and aromas, these vegetables become tasty, palate-teasing creations. And whether it's potatoes, squash or zucchini, the end result is definitely appetizing!

In side dishes, the chili pepper is a star, providing color and awakening flavors, transforming dishes with bright red touches and firing up sometimes neutral tones to boost the taste quotient. Take the turnip: if we remove the aroma of garlic, balanced with notes of the idealino, it would remain a good vegetable, but would you go back for a second forkful? Doubtful!

Among the fruits of the garden, pumpkin's sweet pulp is used often in winter months, but it certainly isn't irresistible. However, cooked with rosemary and chili pepper (choosing between the conquistador, a spicy medium-high pepper vareity, and the dolcevita, which is aromatic and only a little spicy), it comes to life, with color, aromas and liveliness, in the process, becoming a very appetizing dish.

With some creativity, side dishes can be combined into wonderful dishes, as in the case of sweet and sour peppers (a variant of the classic ratatouille), which thanks to the addition of raisins, changes into an interesting mix of sweet, sour, spicy and savory flavors: the chili pepper, in this case, can be delicate, such as the cheiro or yebo, or medium, such as the idealino, or stronger, such as the abbraccio, which is suitable for palates accustomed to a certain amount of spiciness. For the classic ratatouille recipe, it's best to wait for the summer, as you can truly benefit from the maximum flavor of ripe vegetables. You should also remember to use the strong and powerful habanero - choosing between red, orange or chocolate, all with an almost unlimited spiciness - which, used in appropriate doses, provides an intense and appetizing aroma.

Beans, which at one time (and in many places) were often the main course themselves, are not exactly a memorable food, even if they tend to be quite tasty when fresh. Still, in a dish like the Best-Ever Texas Caviar, which seems like a dedication to the traditional cowboy way of life, the pickled jalapeño and yellow Aji habanero provide a strong, robust flavor that feels especially fitting. The red habanero, meanwhile, provides Habanero Red Beans with so much energy, it's best paired with white rice, which can absorb some of its power and ardor.

# BAKED PUMPKIN WITH RED PEPPERS

Difficulty of preparation: Easy - Degree of difficulty: Easy - Preparation time: 5 minutes - Cooking time: 30 minutes

## INGREDIENTS FOR 4 PEOPLE

4 1/3 CUPS (500 G) PUMPKIN

1/2 CUP (50 G) BREAD CRUMBS

2 TO 3 SPRIGS ROSEMARY

2 DOLCEVITA CHILI PEPPERS

EXTRA VIRGIN OLIVE OIL

SALT

Remove the skin, seeds and filaments of the pulp of the pumpkin, then cut into slices just under a half inch thick (1 centimeter). Steam the pumpkin slices for 10 minutes. Then remove them and let them cool on a wooden board.

Wash the chili peppers, dry them, then remove the stem, and, if you want to reduce the spiciness, the seeds. Preheat the oven to 330° F (200° C) Peel the rosemary, wash and then pat dry with
a kitchen towel. Coat the pumpkin slices in bread crumbs and arrange them on the baking sheet. Sprinkle with the rosemary (leave some aside for garnish); chop the chili peppers now, and sprinkle them onto the pumpkin as well. Salt to your liking and drizzle on a few drops of oil.

Bake at 390° F (200°C) for 10 to 15 minutes or until the pumpkin looks inviting and crisp. Remove from the oven, arrange the slices on individual plates, garnishing with the remaining rosemary. Serve hot.

*Baked pumpkin with rosemary and pepper is a light, tasty and appetizing side dish that can complete any table at Halloween, or any time of year. Fruit of the Cucurbitaceous – the plant family that hosts melons, gourds, and squashes – has very sweet and soft flesh, and is ideal to accompany main courses of white meat, such as chicken and turkey or other vegetables and legumes. Its sweetness is balanced finely with the feisty and spicy taste of chili. Pumpkins belonging to the family of cucurbits are native to Central America and have quickly spread around the world thanks to their great adaptability in cultivation and their ease of use in the kitchen. This recipe is also very useful in low calorie diets (only 18 calories per 100 g!). Non-alcoholic beer or fruit juices made from citrus fruits are a great accompaniment to this side dish.*

# PAN ROASTED VEGETABLES

Difficulty of preparation: Easy - Degree of difficulty: Easy - Preparation time: 5 minutes - Cooking time: 25-30 minutes

## INGREDIENTS FOR 2 PEOPLE

14 OZ (400 G) ZUCCHINI

10 1/2 OZ (300 G) CARROTS

1 SMALL ONION

1/4 CUP (60 ML) VEGETABLE BROTH

1 DRIED BACCO CHILI PEPPER

2 TBSP EXTRA VIRGIN OLIVE OIL

SALT

Peel the carrots and cut into slices about 1/10-inch (3 millimeters) thick. Wash the zucchini and slice them like the carrots. Peel and cut the onion. Mash the chili in a mortar.

Bring the broth to a boil and keep hot until ready to use. Heat the oil in a nonstick frying pan and then lower the heat and sauté the onion and half of the ground chili. Cook until the onion is soft but not brown, then add the carrots. Stir and cook uncovered for another 5 minutes, adding spoonfuls of hot broth as needed.

Add the zucchini and continue cooking, adding a tablespoon of broth at a time until the vegetables are at a desired consistency. Add salt to taste. Carefully distribute the chili during cooking so that the spice mixes well with the sweet flavor of the vegetables, particularly the carrots and zucchini. It's an easy-to-make side dish, perfect with white meats like chicken and turkey. If you prefer crispy vegetables, raise the flame when cooked, letting any water evaporate. Serve hot or warm.

*This simple side dish fits in with any main course, be it vegetarian, meat or fish, and is especially suitable for vegetarian diets and any detoxifying efforts. Carrots, with their sugary taste, are well suited to absorb the jolt of hot pepper; zucchini, with their fresh, light taste, provide balance. Carrots and zucchini are also an excellent source of minerals, vitamins and fiber. Add green tea to this treasure trove of nutrients, and you'll also gain antioxidant benefits.*

# SPICY SALAD
# WITH RADICCHIO AND FETA

## INGREDIENTS FOR 4 PEOPLE

3.5 OZ (100 G) RADICCHIO (CHICORY)

3.5 OZ (100 G) FETA CHEESE

2 TO 3 TOMATOES

2 TBSP (17 G) BLACK OLIVES

1 CARROT

1 FRESH ACI SIVRI CHILI PEPPER

1 FRESH YEBO CHILI PEPPER

4 STEMS OF CHIVES

6 TBSP (90 ML) EXTRA VIRGIN OLIVE OIL

Peel and carefully wash the radicchio, tomatoes and the chilies, then dry with paper towels. Gently wash the chives, pat it dry with a kitchen towel and chop finely. Wash and peel the carrot and cut into matchsticks.

Slice the tomatoes into wedges, the radicchio into thin strips, the black olives into slices and, handling with great care (it's a good idea to use latex gloves), finely chop the chilies. Dice the feta cheese. Pour the oil into a bowl, add salt to taste and chili pepper, stir and leave aside until ready to use.

At serving time, place the tomato slices as a base on each individual plate, then the radicchio, olives, cheese, and carrot shreds, and season with chives. Drizzle with the chili oil to taste (and to your ability to handle spice) or serve the oil separately.

*This is a very fresh salad that can be served as a side dish and, in larger servings, as a main course, particularly in warm weather. Fragrant, spicy and aromatic, it is a great combination of tasty ingredients that is also an interesting source of nutrients, including the vitamins and minerals contained in the tomatoes; the fibers of the chicory; and the calcium and phosphorus of the feta. We are not accustomed to thinking of food as the structure of our cells, we consider it a pleasure more than anything. But in this case, a recipe can become an ally, providing light, easily digestible and nutritious food that is also delicious. A few handy tips: always use ripe tomatoes, fresh and healthy radicchio and carrots peeled only at the time of use. A warm or cold tea made from mint is the best beverage with which to accompany this salad.*

# SPICY BROCCOLI RAAB

Difficulty of preparation: Easy - Degree of difficulty: Easy - Preparation time: 35 minutes - Cooking time: 25-30 minutes - Resting time: 30 minutes

## INGREDIENTS FOR 2 PEOPLE

14 OZ (400 G) BROCCOLI RAAB
1 CLOVE GARLIC
5 2/3 OZ (160 G) CHERRY TOMATOES
1 DRIED IDEALINO CHILI PEPPER

1 SPRIG OF ROSEMARY
2 TBSP (30 ML) EXTRA VIRGIN OLIVE OIL
SALT

Chop the broccoli raab, removing tough stems and any leathery leaves. Soak it in cold water for about 30 minutes, then rinse well. Steam the greens for about 10 to 15 minutes – longer if you prefer it softer, less if you want it on the crisp side.

Meanwhile, wash the tomatoes and bring 4 cups (1 liter) of salted water to boil. Drop the tomatoes into the water to cook for 1 minute, then collect them with a slotted spoon.
Cut them into halves or quarters, depending on their size, but don't peel them.

Strip the rosemary from the stem and chop finely. Peel and crush the garlic, and grind the chili in a mortar. For a very spicy dish, include the seeds; otherwise, take them out. Heat the oil in a large saucepan and sauté the garlic, rosemary, and half the pepper. When the garlic starts to brown, add the tomatoes. Cook over medium heat for about 5 minutes, then increase the heat to high and add the broccoli. Cook for 2 minutes more. Season with salt and more chili pepper to your taste. Remove from heat, stir, and transfer to a serving dish. Serve hot or at room temperature.

*Spicy broccoli raab is a tasty side dish typical of Apulia (the region is the heel of Italy's "boot"). It's a very simple recipe and traditional "peasant" fare. At one time this nutritious vegetable was a frequent substitute for meat, which was much more expensive. In addition to being an excellent side dish, spicy broccoli raab can also be tossed with pasta. A glass of red wine is its ideal companion.*

# SWISS CHARD WITH ORANGE

Difficulty of preparation: Easy - Degree of difficulty: Easy - Preparation time: 15 minutes - Cooking time: 10-15 minutes

## INGREDIENTS FOR 4 PEOPLE

25 OZ (700 G) OF CHARD
1 SMALL ORGANIC ORANGE
1 ORGANIC LEMON
2 CLOVES GARLIC
1 DRIED VIGEI CHILI PEPPER
4 TBSP (60 ML) EXTRA VIRGIN OLIVE OIL
SALT

Wash the citrus and dry them with paper towels. Using a lemon zester, remove the peel from the citrus. Pay attention to the white part, which should not be kept. Grind the chili pepper in a mortar. Clean and wash the chard, rinsing several times in running water. Finally, drain it, dry it and cut it to a size you want.

Heat the oil in a wok, peel and crush the garlic and sauté. When browned, add the zest (reserving about a quarter of it for decoration), part of the chili pepper and the chard. Sauté for a few minutes over high heat, adding salt to taste, and checking that the level of spiciness is to your taste. Add more pepper if necessary. Cook on high heat for about 8 to 10 minutes, stirring constantly with a wooden spoon.

Add the lemon juice to the chard. Combine well to mix the flavors and turn off the heat. Distribute in individual plates, decorating with citrus zest and serve to the table piping hot.

*Swiss chard is a herbaceous plant known since ancient times. It is very nutritious, containing minerals, vitamin C and carotenoids, which our bodies turn into vitamin A. It is also believed that the presence of chlorophyll can also protect against cancer. A simple green vegetable, therefore, it is very easy to prepare and can be enjoyed 2-3 times a week, especially during the colder months of the year. Tangerine and orange juice is the drink with which to enrich the benefits of this simple and healthy dish.*

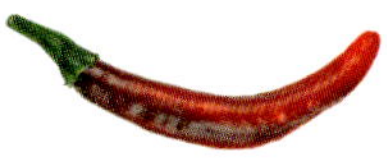

# SLICED POTATOES IN SWEET AND SOUR SAUCE

*Difficulty of preparation: Easy - Degree of difficulty: Easy - Preparation time: 10 minutes - Cooking time: 20-25 minutes - Resting time: 20 minutes*

## INGREDIENTS FOR 4 PEOPLE

4 YELLOW POTATOES

1 GREEN PEPPER

1 BUNCH OF PARSLEY

10 STEMS OF CHIVES

4 TO 5 DRIED BELVIOLA CHILI PEPPERS

2 TBSP (30 ML) WINE VINEGAR

6 TBSP (90 ML) OLIVE OIL

SALT

Wash the potatoes, brush the skin and boil for 20 minutes, then drain and let cool on a wooden board. Meanwhile, wash and chop the parsley. Place the chilis in a damp kitchen towel and grind them in a mortar. Wash the green pepper, then remove the stem and the white part attached to the seeds and cut into small pieces. Rinse the chives, dry them, and chop finely.

Pour oil, vinegar, chives, chili and parsley in a bowl, salt to taste and stir. Add the green pepper and let sit for 20 minutes, stirring occasionally.

When the potatoes are at room temperature, slice (without peeling) using a sharp knife (to ensure that the potatoes don't adhere to the blade, rinse it often with water). Arrange on plates and drizzle with the marinade. Serve cold as a salad or as an appetizer.

*This recipe combines the cooking habits of Nordic countries with the Mediterranean for an excellent result! Fresh, light and easily digestible, sweet and sour potatoes are a perfect complement to dishes based on mutton and lamb. They are, however, also a wonderful appetizer. Potatoes belong to the Solanaceae family, originating in Ameria. They are a staple food that has spread all over the world. Very nutritious, they can easily substitute pasta or bread. An equally weighted portion, however, has a much smaller amount of calories. This recipe, therefore, is great for low-calorie diets. A glass of red wine is the perfect drink to emphasize the sweetness of the potatoes and the freshness of the sauce.*

# ITALIAN PEPPER STEW WITH HABANERO

## INGREDIENTS FOR 4 PEOPLE

1 RED PEPPER

1 YELLOW PEPPER

1 GREEN PEPPER

1 FRESH HABANERO CHILI PEPPER (TO YOUR TASTE)

1 RED ONION

2 TBSP (17 G) SALTED CAPERS

1 TBSP (3 G) DRIED OREGANO

4 TBSP (60 ML) EXTRA VIRGIN OLIVE OIL

SALT

Wash the peppers, remove the stem, seeds and white parts and cut into slices. Pass a damp cloth over the chili pepper and finely chop half of it. Cut the remainder into rings that will be used to decorate the plate (always carefully handle habanero peppers with latex gloves and avoid touching your face). Peel and finely slice the onion. Soak the capers in warm water and rinse repeatedly to remove the salt, then dry them with a towel and let them sit in a colander for 5 minutes.

Heat the oil in a frying pan and cook the onion over low heat to soften it. After a few minutes add the crushed chili. When the onion begins to soften, add the bell peppers and half the oregano. Simmer, covered, for about 30 minutes, making sure the cooking liquid does not evaporate too much. If it does, add a few tablespoons of hot water and reduce the heat to the minimum. Check the salt before removing it from the heat.

Transfer to a serving dish, flavor with the remaining oregano, the capers and the habanero rings. Serve warm or at room temperature.

*Dedicated to lovers of peppers, this full immersion in color and flavor is an unforgettable dish, a sort of "Italian Ratatouille". Keeping the original color of the peppers, and maintaining the versatile and irresistible aroma of Mediterranean flavors, it's perfect as a side dish, complimenting more delicate meat dishes, boiled vegetables and rice. However, this dish can also be very enjoyable with just a few slices of crusty bread. A glass of light, moderately chilled red wine is the best wine to complement this spicy pepper stew.*

# VARIATION OF PEPPERS WITH RAISINS

Difficulty of preparation: Easy - Degree of difficulty: Easy - Preparation time: 10 minutes - Cooking time: 25-30 minutes - Resting time: 5 minutes

## INGREDIENTS FOR 4 PEOPLE

1 RED PEPPER

1 YELLOW PEPPER

3/4 CUP (200 G) OF TOMATO PULP

1 TO 2 DRIED IDEALINO CHILI PEPPERS

  (TO YOUR TASTE)

1 RED ONION

2 TBSP (30 G) RAISINS

2 TBSP (30 ML) EXTRA VIRGIN

  OLIVE OIL

SALT

To prepare the recipe, first wash the peppers, then remove the stems, seeds, and the white parts. Wash and finely chop the chili pepper. Peel and finely slice the red onion. Soak the raisins in a glass of warm water, then drain well.

Pour oil into a heavy-bottomed saucepan, add the onion, then add the crushed red pepper. When the onion begins to soften, add the peppers, the tomatoes, and the carefully drained raisins. Add salt to taste and cook over low heat for about 20 minutes, stirring occasionally.

Check the seasoning, adding salt and more chili pepper if you like – it depends on your ability to handle spice. Let stand the mixture covered for 5 minutes. Then serve hot or warm.

*This pepper recipe is a variant of a classic Italian side dish that has numerous regional variations: capers in the islands, tomatoes in the center of the country and garlic to the north. In all parts of the peninsula, however, it is an irresistible side dish that can be served hot, warm or cold. Used to accompany meat, fish and white rice, it can even be enjoyed by itself. It is also useful as part of a low-calorie diet and very nutritious, with a large amount of nutrients that help promote well-being, including: beta carotene, vitamin C, antioxidant, B vitamins. A slightly chilled, light-bodied red wine is the recommended drink.*

# SPICY CAULIFLOWER DAL

## INGREDIENTS FOR 4 PEOPLE

| | |
|---|---|
| 1 1/8 PLBS (500 G) CAULIFLOWER | 2 BAY LEAVES |
| 1 CUP (200 G) RED LENTILS | 1 TBSP (7 G) TURMERIC POWDER |
| 2 ONIONS | 1 TBSP (7 G) GROUND CUMIN |
| 4 TOMATOES | 1 TBSP (7 G) GARAM MASALA (SPICE MIXTURE) |
| 1 GREEN PEPPER | 3 SPRIGS FRESH CILANTRO |
| 1 AJI COLORADO CHILI PEPPER | 4 CUPS HOT WATER |
| 4 TBSP (60 ML) GHEE (CLARIFIED BUTTER) | SALT |

Wash the lentils under running water several times. Blanch the tomatoes and remove the skin, then cut them into cubes and remove the seeds. Peel the onions and cut them into small pieces. Wash the peppers, removing the stems, seeds, and white parts. Cut what's left into pieces. Wash and cut the chili peppers into 2 parts lengthwise. Pass the cilantro under running water, dry gently and remove the hard parts.

Sauté the onions in a pan with the ghee and stir frequently; when golden, add the red pepper, bay leaves, turmeric and cumin, and cook over medium heat for 2 minutes stirring constantly. Add the cauliflower, tomatoes, green pepper and lentils. Pour the hot water into the pan, bring to a boil and cook, covered, over medium heat for about 25 minutes. Salt to taste.

When cooked, remove from heat, stir in the garam masala, and make individual dishes, seasoning each one with fresh cilantro. Serve.

*This dish, which originated in India, is a triumph of aromas, flavors and spices that enhance and emphasize the potential taste of the vegetables involved. It's a rich side dish that can accompany white rice, wheat, beans and pepper bread, but also beef stew, stewed lamb, goat and sheep. Nevertheless, it can also be a main dish. The ideal drink for this recipe should be aromatic, robust and spiced, like a full-bodied sauvignon blanc from Australia.*

# CHAO HELANDOU
# (SWEET AND SOUR GREEN BEANS)

Difficulty of preparation: Easy - Degree of difficulty: Easy - Preparation time: 7-10 minutes - Cooking time: 12 minutes

## INGREDIENTS FOR 4 PEOPLE

2 1/4 LBS (1 KG) SWEET GREEN BEANS

4 CLOVES GARLIC

2 DRIED TABASCO CHILI PEPPERS

4 TBSP (60 ML) SOYBEAN OIL

1 CUP (240 ML) HOT WATER

2 TBSP (30 ML) SOY SAUCE

2 TBSP (30 ML) SAKE

Peel the beans and trim the ends. If they are very long, break it up so that you have numerous pieces of more or less the same length. Rinse and drain in a colander. Peel the garlic, cut into thin strips and marinate in soy sauce for about 10 minutes. Clean the chilies with a damp towel, then chop finely.

Pour the oil into a wok and fry the chilies (if you do not have this type of pan, use a nonstick frying pan); add the garlic marinated in soy sauce, the beans and stir. Fry for 2 minutes on high heat, then add the water. Cover, reduce the heat and let soften for about 8 minutes.

Check that everything is well cooked, add the soy used for marinating the garlic and the sake. Evaporate and reduce at high heat, them remove from the stove and make individual dishes. Serve hot or warm.

*This recipe from China is a refined, aromatic side dish full of flavor. The balance of the various ingredients softens the tones of the garlic and red pepper and enhances the fresh lightness of the green beans. For the preparation of the dish you can use either sugar or snow peas, green beans from Kenya, dolichos asparagus, or snap peas. The important thing is the freshness and crispness of the vegetables. A perfect side dish for fish or fried foods, it is ideally served hot or warm, but it can also be enjoyed as a cold appetizer. Ales and dry white wines are the perfect complement to the dish.*

# BEST-EVER TEXAS CAVIAR

Difficulty of preparation: Easy - Degree of difficulty: Easy - Preparation time: 10 minutes - Cooking time: 5 minutes - Resting time: 5 minutes

## INGREDIENTS FOR 4 PEOPLE

1 SMALL CAN OF BLACK BEANS

1 SMALL CAN OF KIDNEY BEANS

1 SMALL CAN OF WHITE CORN

2 GREEN JALAPEÑO CHILI PEPPERS IN BRINE

1 AJI CHILI PEPPER

1 RED BELVIOLA CHILI PEPPER

1 RED BELL PEPPER

1 SMALL ONION

1 BUNCH FRESH CILANTRO

1/2 CUP (120 ML) RICE VINEGAR

1/2 CUP (120 ML) OLIVE OIL

1/3 CUP (70 G) WHITE SUGAR

1/2 TEASPOON (1 1/2 G) POWDERED GARLIC

SALT

Drain the canned beans and corn, wash them to remove any water; let them drain in a colander and pour into a bowl. Clean the red bell pepper, removing the stems, seeds and white parts and cut into small cubes. Slice the green jalapeño peppers. Wash the other chili peppers (using latex gloves), then remove the seeds and stems and cut all this into very small pieces. Add to beans.

Rinse the cilantro, patting it dry with paper towels, then finely chop 2/3; pour in the beans and leave the most beautiful leaves for decoration. Peel and slice the onion finely and add it to other ingredients in the bowl. Prepare the dressing by mixing oil, vinegar, sugar and garlic in a bowl. Bring to boil, then remove from heat and let it cool.

When the sauce has cooled, add it to the vegetables, salt to taste, and stir gently to avoid damaging the beans, then transfer to individual plates and flavor with the remaining cilantro.

*Originally from Texas, this delicious, flavorful and easy to prepare dish is dedicated to the hard life of the "cowboy"! Best Ever Texas Caviar is a very nutritious dish that can easily substitute animal protein. It is great as an accompaniment to sausages and rice, but also works well with hot tortillas. Beer is the best beverage with which to appreciate this dish.*

# HABANERO RED BEANS

## INGREDIENTS FOR 4 PEOPLE

1 FRESH RED HABANERO PEPPER

1 CAN OF BEANS IN BRINE

1 SMALL RED ONION

1 SMALL RED BELL PEPPER

7 OZ (200 G) TOMATO SAUCE

3 TBSP (45 ML) EXTRA VIRGIN OLIVE OIL

SALT

It's always advisable to handle habanero peppers with gloves and never touch your face, as their concentrated capsaicin can inflame the skin and mucous membranes! Wash the habanero thoroughly and cut into thin strips. Peel the onion and chop finely. Wash the peppers, remove seeds and white parts and cut it into cubes. Pour oil into a saucepan, and over high heat, sauté the peppers and onions. When they start to soften, add the tomato sauce. Add salt to taste and continue cooking over low heat.

Drain the beans and rinse them under running water to remove any residual fluid. When the tomato sauce begins to thicken, add the red habanero, as much or as little as you'd like. Keep in mind that it does not take much to infuse a dish with its intense heat. Continue cooking for a few minutes and then add the beans. Add more salt to taste, if desired. Keep on medium heat for a few more minutes, stirring frequently.

Remove from heat, pouring the beans in individual bowls and serving with corn chips.

*This is a very spicy dish, and very good with steamed basmati rice, which is capable of balancing the spice and exuberance of chili peppers. The pepper's name is believed to have been derived from the name of Cuba's capital, Havana. Those who are just getting acquainted with this strong pepper should build up their tolerance to its heat by adding it to recipes gradually. Red habanero beans are an excellent main course as well, and many drinks can enhance it, including beer, tequila and rum.*

# ADS BI DERSA
# (LENTILS IN SPICY SAUCE)

Difficulty of preparation: Easy - Degree of difficulty: Easy - Resting time: 8 hours - Preparation time: 5 minutes - Cooking time: circa: 30 minutes

## INGREDIENTS FOR 4 PEOPLE

2 2/3 CUPS (500 G) LENTILS

1 ONION

2 BAY LEAVES

2 CLOVES GARLIC

2 DRIED BODY GUARD CHILI PEPPERS, CHOPPED

1 PINCH OF CINNAMON

1 TSP (2 G) OF CUMIN

4 TBSP (60 ML) EXTRA VIRGIN OLIVE OIL

4 PIECES UNLEAVENED BREAD

SALT AND PEPPERCORNS

Rinse the lentils and soak them in cold water for 8 hours. Drain and rinse again, then boil them in salted water for 10 minutes; drain, and set aside. Remove the outer layers of the onion and chop finely. Peel and crush the garlic with the tines of a fork.

In a bowl, stir the garlic, chili pepper, salt, ground pepper, cinnamon and cumin.
Pour the oil into a nonstick skillet, brown the onion, add the spices, bay leaf, lentils and 3 1/3 cups (800 milliliters) of water. Bring to a boil, stir and cook over low heat for 20 minutes.

Just before removing from the heat, adjust the salt, remove the bay leaves, and thicken any resulting liquid (if necessary) by increasing the flame. Remove from heat. Let cool. Pour the seasoning into the bowl and stir so that the ingredients are well combined. Serve at room temperature, accompanying the dish with slices of unleavened bread heated in the oven a few moments earlier.

*The recipe of Algerian origins can be either served as a side dish with other vegetables, pasta and rice or as a complete meal with unleavened bread. Lentils, a good substitute for animal protein, is an essential food, especially for people who give up meat. They are indeed very rich in essential amino acids and have a fair amount of minerals, such as iron, phosphorus, zinc and calcium. You can accompany the dish with any herb-flavored tea, hot and sweet.*

# STUFFED MEXICAN PEPPERS

Difficulty of preparation: Easy - Degree of difficulty: Medium - Preparation time: 10 minutes - Cooking time: 35 minutes

## INGREDIENTS FOR 4 PEOPLE

6 MEDIUM GREEN PEPPERS

3.5 OZ (100 G) WHITE RICE

3.5 OZ (100 G) FENNEL SAUSAGE

1 DRIED FATALII CHILI PEPPER

3.5 OZ (100 G) TOMATO PUREE

1 EGG

OLIVE OIL

SALT

Boil the rice in salted water until al dente, then drain and season with 2 tablespoons of olive oil to prevent the grains from sticking together. Wash the peppers and cut horizontally at 2/3 of the height in order to create a container. This way you can also easily remove the seeds and white parts (leave the stem). With your hands, coat the inside and outside of the peppers with oil. Remove the sausage casing.

In a bowl, mix the rice with the sausage, egg, half the chilies (crushed at the time of cooking) and a tablespoon of tomato puree. Salt to taste and stir until the different ingredients are well mixed together. Stuff the half peppers.

Preheat the oven to 350° F (180° C). Line a baking sheet with waxed paper and arrange the peppers on it. Spread a little tomato puree on the fillings and bake for about 20 minutes, then check that the filling is thoroughly cooked and remove from oven. When ready to serve, remove the peppers from the oven, transfer to a serving dish. Serve warm or at room temperature.

*Stuffed peppers are a traditional Italian and Mexican dish that can be stuffed with vegetables, meat or cheese. Seemingly unconnected, the Italian and Mexican versions of this dish share many flavors, though both add their own touches, depending on the ingredients that are most readily available. Normally served to accompany main courses, they can also be used as an appetizer or stuffed with other vegetables, such as potatoes, onions and tomatoes (a veritable triumph of stuffing!) They are a complete and delicious food that can get people salivating on sight. A very cold beer or sparkling white wine are recommended.*

# SAUCES AND PRESERVES

Our journey takes us into the world of spicy sauces and compotes, which are sometimes needed as more than just an accompaniment to important dishes, acting as a flavor booster. Take the Mexican mole poblano: it is a condiment that, according to tradition, is prepared with at least 50 different ingredients. This sauce can transform any dish into an explosion of taste, with the orange habanero's power playing a key role by tying all the components together.

Also from the land of the Aztecs, we get guacamole, a preparation that can turn just about any taco into a tasty, appetizing treat. With a captivating green color, guacamole offers a balanced mix between the sweet pulp of the avocado, the sourness of the tomatoes and the spice from the jalapeño, which gives the sauce that world famous harmony and flavor.

Tomatillo, with its firm texture and fresh and juicy taste, is perfect with a touch of green acrobata. Also from Mexico, where spice is ubiquitous, come a variety of chili pepper salsas. Just add crunchy nachos for dipping, and enjoy.

We jump to North Africa continent with the recipe for hummus, a delicious sauce made from mashed chickpeas sprinkled with toasted sesame, a special flavor made even more intriguing by the presence of the Azerbaijan pepper, a not too spicy variety that provides a sweet taste that complements the velvety texture of the preparation. The soft but fiery character of the harissa sauce, meanwhile, is made of garlic, seeds, fragrant herbs, sweet peppers and the chili pepper that gives the sauce its name (intensity will depend on how you prepare the peppers – with seeds and veins or without).

Taking our cue from Turkey, we prepare a preserve that can enrich winter dishes with flavors and scents of summer: eggplants and nuts, seasoned with a pinch of cayenne powder and a aci sivri chili pepper; let it sit in olive oil, remove it and chop, mixing it with vegetables and sauces to enhance the flavor of meat and pasta dishes.

From Italy, meanwhle, comes the pilacca, which is brilliant with fresh vegetables cut into small pieces; let it sit in vinegar, then preserve it in oil, using it as a seasoning to flavor dishes and prepare tasty bruschetta! Of course, this should go without saying, as the chili pepper is an essential ingredient for flavoring vegetables, enlivening them with spicy notes. The fueguitos pepper, which is as beautiful as it is tasty, is particularly useful in this regard.

Now let's fly back home to start the BBQ, a style of cooking that would lose much of its personality without the Caribbean Barbecue Sauce, a complex set of tastes, spices and herbs that requires a balance of ingredients; the tabasco pepper creates the right balance between sweet and sour, regulating the overall exuberance of the spices so that the aromatic spiciness does not overpower the other flavors.

Finally, we move to India for the basic curry sauce, the wonderfully spicy, fragrant and appetizing sauce use to make chicken, rice and vegetable delicacies. The preparation (bolstered by the strong flavor of cayenne) is a veritable kaleidoscope of tastes, which, taken together, tells the colorful history of Indian cuisine. Even in the case of fig chutney, spice tones are the theme of the compound. Still, the Indian chili pepper offers the perfect balance of flavors for any kind of meat dish.

# SPICY GREEN SAUCE WITH CAPERS

*Difficulty of preparation: Easy - Preparation time: 25-30 minutes*

## INGREDIENTS FOR 4 PEOPLE

1 SALTED ANCHOVY

1/4 CUP (30 G) WHITE BREAD CRUMBS

2 CLOVES GARLIC

3/4 CUP + 2 TBSP (50 G) FRESH PARSLEY

3/4 CUP + 2 TBSP (200 ML) EXTRA VIRGIN OLIVE OIL

2 TBSP + 1 TSP (20 G) SALTED CAPERS

3 1/3 TBSP (50 ML) WINE VINEGAR

2 FRESH ALFIERE CHILI PEPPERS

SALT

Desalt the capers by soaking them in warm water, then wash, drain and chop them. Peel and chop the garlic. Clean the parsley, remove the stems and chop the leaves. Put the capers, garlic, and parsley together in a bowl that will be large enough to hold all the ingredients.

Rinse the anchovy in cold water to remove some of the salt. Filet the fish, then mince it and add it to the bowl with the parsley. Combine the bread crumbs and vinegar in a small bowl and let it stand for 5 minutes. Squeeze out the excess vinegar and add the bread crumbs to the parsley bowl. Wash the alfiere chili peppers. Chop one of them finely and cut the other into thin, round slices.

Combine the chopped parsley, finely cut chili pepper, salt to taste and a drizzle of oil, stirring vigorously so that the ingredients blend together perfectly. Pour the mixture into a sauce boat and decorate with the round slices of alfiere chili pepper. Garnish with sprigs of parsley and serve at room temperature. Accompanies both hot and cold dishes.

*This sauce is decidedly tasty, as well as fresh, harmonious and complex due to the ingredients that it is made with. In Piedmont, especially in areas of Langhe and Monferrato, it is nearly always served alongside boiled eggs, green-style anchovies, tongue, and many other dishes that are traditional in the region. Although the chili pepper is not an ingredient in the original recipe, it's a welcome update in this never-fail, Sunday dinner condiment.*

# MOLE POBLANO
# (SAUCE FROM PUEBLA)

## INGREDIENTS FOR 4 PEOPLE

1 ORANGE HABANERO CHILI PEPPER

1 BIG JIM CHILI PEPPER

2/5 CUP (60 G) SESAME SEEDS

3 TBSP (25 G) BLANCHED ALMONDS

2 TBSP (20 G) SHELLED PEANUTS

1 ONION

1 CLOVE GARLIC

1/4 CUP (40 G) TOMATO PULP

1/8 CUP (20 G) RAISINS

1 SMALL BANANA

1 TSP (2 G) GROUND CLOVE

1 TSP (2 G) CORIANDER SEEDS

1 TSP (2 G) FENNEL SEEDS

1 3/4 OZ (50 G) UNSWEETENED CHOCOLATE

1 TBSP (12.5 G) SUGAR

2 TBSP (30 ML) OIL

Toast the sesame seeds, almonds and peanuts. On a chopping board, crumble the chocolate with a knife. Peel the onion and garlic and chop finely. Peel the banana and cut into round slices. Remove the stalk, seeds and white parts of the peppers, then steam until the outer skins change color and peel off. Soak the peppers in water, drain, pat dry with paper towels, and chop finely.

Pour the oil into a nonstick skillet, sauté the onion and garlic, then add the peppers, sesame seeds, peanuts, almonds, banana slices, raisins and the spices. Combine well, then add the tomato pulps chocolate and sugar. Simmer on low heat for about 1 hour, then blend finely.

Serve the sauce warm or hot with turkey, chicken or white rice.

*Mole is an Aztec word and refers to an aromatic and spicy sauce. The creation of mole poblano is attributed to the nuns of the convent of Santa Rosa in Puebla, Mexico, and in order to make a dish worthy of a visit from the viceroy himself, they used up all the resources from the pantry. Thus was born a very special and particularly spicy sauce with which to enrich and serve with any ingredient. Tradition has it that they are at least 50 ingredients that make up the specialty (we saved you quite a few!). There are many versions, such as with broth, bacon, and corn flour. For a first approach, using this sauce adds plenty of flavor to neutral foods such as chicken and rice, which are able to accommodate the complexity of the sauce, but it's also great on vegetables and fruit.*

# GUACAMOLE

*Difficulty of preparation: Easy - Degree of difficulty: Medium - Preparation time: 10 minutes*

## INGREDIENTS FOR 4 PEOPLE

2 RIPE AVOCADOS

1 MEDIUM SWEET ONION

1 FIRM, RIPE TOMATO

2 JALAPEÑO CHILI PEPPERS

2 SPRIGS OF CILANTRO

1 LIME

SALT

Choose avocados that yield slightly to a gentle squeeze. The skins should have no loose or brown spots. Slice them in half lengthwise and twist to separate the halves. Remove the pit. Scoop the avocado out of the peel, put it in a bowl and mash it with a fork. It may take longer this way than using a food processor, but the texture is worth every minute!

Peel and finely chop the onion. Peel and seed the tomato, then cut into very small pieces. Slice the jalapeños chili peppers into thin strips, wearing gloves to avoid irritating the skin, and chop the cilantro.

Combine all the ingredients with the avocado and add salt to taste, then squeeze the lime juice into the guacamole a little at a time. Taste for seasoning, and combine well but gently. Garnish with a couple of pepper slices and a sliver of lime, and refrigerate until ready to serve.

*In traditional Mexican guacamole, lime juice is a key ingredient. Some European recipes call for lemon juice instead, but it doesn't have quite the same snap. Either way, guacamole is a treat. Serve it with corn chips, tortillas, or white meats. Add a very salty margarita for a match made in heaven. Avocados brown quickly when exposed to air, so enjoy your guacamole while it's very very fresh!*

# BASIC CURRY SAUCE

## INGREDIENTS FOR 4 PEOPLE

1 ONION

1 CUP (250 ML) SOY MILK

1 TBSP (5 G) POWDERED CAYENNE CHILI PEPPER

3 TBSP (20 G) GROUND TURMERIC

4 TBSP (20 G) DRIED CORIANDER SEEDS

1 OZ (30 G) FRESH GINGER

3 1/2 (20 G) GROUND CARDAMOM

3 1/3 TBSP (20 G) CUMIN SEEDS

2 TBSP (10 G) FENUGREEK SEEDS

1 TBSP (8 G) ALL-PURPOSE FLOUR

2 TBSP (30 ML) EXTRA VIRGIN OLIVE OIL

SALT

Grate the ginger and collect the juice and pulp. In a mortar, pound the coriander, cumin and fenugreek seeds into a fine powder.

Peel the onion and chop finely. Pour the oil in a skillet and when hot, brown the onions on medium heat. As soon as they become golden and soft, sift the flour into the pan and stir. Immediately add the milk and stir continuously to avoid the formation of lumps.

As soon as the mixture begins to boil, stir in coriander, cumin and fenugreek powder, add the other ground spices, the ginger, and chili pepper. Mix well to blend the flavors. Add salt to taste. Leave to heat for a few minutes and if the sauce is too thick, add some more soy milk by the spoonful.

*"Curry" derives from the Tamil word* cari, *which means sauce. In fact, in Indian cuisine, this mixture of spices called a* masala. *Ready-made curry powders are widely available, but their flavors can't compare to a blend prepared at home. Plus, by making your own, you can fiddle with the ingredients to concoct a combination that suits your taste, or the cuisine, perfectly. Curry is perfect for preparing particularly aromatic rice dishes, for seasoning meats and fishes, as a spread on toasts, and even as a dressing for salads, vegetables, or boiled potatoes.*

# CARIBBEAN BARBECUE SAUCE

## INGREDIENTS FOR 4 PEOPLE

6 SCALLIONS, SLICED THIN, WHITE PARTS ONLY

1 SHALLOT, MINCED

2 CLOVES GARLIC, MINCED

1 TSP (2 G) GROUND GINGER

1 TBSP (8 G) BODY GUARD CHILI PEPPER, MINCED

2 TABASCO CHILI PEPPERS

1 TBSP (8 G) GROUND CINNAMON

1/2 TSP (1 G) GROUND NUTMEG

1 TBSP (6 G) RAW CANE SUGAR

1 TSP (2 G) GROUND BLACK PEPPER

JUICE OF 1 ORANGE

  (ABOUT 1/4 CUP / 60 MILLILITERS)

3 1/3 TBSP (50 ML) APPLE CIDER VINEGAR

3 1/3 TBSP (50 ML) RED WINE

1 TBSP + 2 TSP (24 ML) SOY SAUCE

3 1/3 TBSP (50 ML) VEGETABLE OIL

1 TBSP (15 ML) MOLASSES

SALT

Clean the green onions by removing the outer leaves and cutting the tips of the green ends, then wash and slice the roots. Peel the scallion and garlic and chop them finely. Wash and peel the ginger, then grate to collect the pulp and juice. Wash the Tabasco peppers, remove the stems and seeds and chop finely.

Squeeze the orange into a medium bowl and add the ginger, the minced body guard chili pepper, the scallions, shallot, peppers, garlic, cinnamon, nutmeg, brown sugar, black pepper, vinegar, wine, soy sauce, oil, and molasses. Season with salt to taste. Mix well, cover and refrigerate for at least 1 hour before using.

The sauce can be served with salads, or drizzled over meat and fish – in fact, for almost any kind of white meat, from pork and duck to chicken or turkey. It will keep, refrigerated, for several days without losing its pronounced flavor and enticing aroma.

*The flavor combinations in this marinade originate from the West Indies. It's possible that the Arawaks native to the islands might have used something like it to flavor fish and game. Naturally, the ingredients have changed with the times, but it's still a great choice for many grilled white meats.*

# MEXICAN SALSA

## INGREDIENTS FOR 4 PEOPLE

4 LARGE TOMATOES

2 MEDIUM WHITE ONIONS, MINCED

2 GARLIC CLOVES, MINCED

2 ACRATA CHILI PEPPERS

1 GREEN JALAPEÑO CHILI PEPPER

1 SPRIG CILANTRO

1 TSP (4 G) CANE SUGAR

2 LIMES

SALT

Peel and seed the tomatoes. One of the easiest methods is to core the tomatoes at the top end and cut an X into the bottom. Bring a large pot of water to boil and slip the tomatoes into the water just until the skin starts to wrinkle (within 30 seconds). Remove the tomatoes with a slotted spoon and immerse them into ice water to stop the cooking. After another 15 to 30 seconds, take the tomatoes out of the ice water. The skins will slip off easily. Open the tomatoes (with a knife or just with your hands), remove the seeds, and dice the tomato pulp. Place into a strainer and let drain for about 5 minutes, then transfer to a large bowl. Wash and chop the cilantro (keep some leaves for garnish).

Wash the chili peppers, remove seeds and white parts, then mince them and add them to the tomatoes, along with the cilantro, onion, garlic and sugar. Juice the limes. Season the salsa with salt and lime juice to taste, then cover and refrigerate for about 1 hour. Garnish with whole cilantro leaves. Serve this salsa alongside grilled meats and sausages or with toasted bread or tortillas.

It makes sense that this blend of ripe red tomatoes, spicy green peppers, and piquant white onions and garlic is known as *Salsa Mexicana* – with all the colors of the Mexican flag, these simple ingredients combine to create something fresh, juicy, intense, inviting, classic, and unforgettable. Magnificent on crusty bread like bruschetta, but also a welcome companion to meat and fish, the flavors are refreshing. Somehow, the spiciness seems to relieve the heat of even the muggiest summer day.

*The peppers' flavonoids and capsaicinoids have antibacterial properties that were much needed in hot climates before the days of refrigeration; they are antifermentative, too, thus helping digestion.*

# TOMATILLO SALSA

Difficulty of preparation: Medium - Degree of difficulty: Medium - Preparation time: 30-40 minutes - Resting time: 5-8 minutes

## INGREDIENTS FOR 4 PEOPLE

1 LBS (ABOUT 500 G) TOMATILLOS,
    SKINNED AND SEEDED
4 CLOVES GARLIC, MINCED
1 SMALL ONION, CHOPPED
2 GREEN ACROBATA CHILI PEPPERS

2/3 CUP (10 G) FRESH CILANTRO, MINCED
2 TBSP (30 ML) OLIVE OIL
2 TSP (12 G) SALT
2 TSP (8 G) SUGAR
2 TBSP (30 ML) WATER

Peel and seed the tomatillos, then chop them. Put them in a small bowl with the garlic and 2/3 of the onion, and set aside. Wash the chili peppers, remove seeds and white parts, then mince them.

Heat the oil in a saucepan over high heat. When it shimmers, add the tomatillo mixture, chili peppers, sugar, salt and water to the pan. Stir continuously and let the sauce reduce, keeping the heat on high, for about 5 minutes.

Remove from heat. Let cool, stir in the cilantro and transfer to a serving dish. Sprinkle with the remaining onion, and serve with bread, breadsticks, or tortillas. Its spicy/tart taste goes very well with pork and chicken.

*There are several variations of this green salsa made from Mexican tomatillos – which are not, in fact, unripe tomatoes, but rather a close relative. In some versions, the ingredients are whisked together for a creamy result; in others, components are roasted before they're combined, which takes out some of the tartness and adds a smoky note. Or, with a lot of patience and a sharp knife, you can mince the ingredients as we do here! In any case, this special sauce can be stored in the fridge for a few days.*

# PICO DE GALLO SALSA

Difficulty of preparation: Easy - Degree of difficulty: Easy - Preparation time: 20 minutes - Resting time: 60 minutes

## INGREDIENTS FOR 4 PEOPLE

4 FIRM, RIPE TOMATOES, SEEDED AND DICED

1 MEDIUM RED ONION

1 FRESH JALAPEÑO CHILI PEPPER

1 BEBEBE CHILI PEPPER

1 1/4 CUPS (20 G) FRESH CILANTRO LEAVES

JUICE OF 1 LIME (ABOUT 2 TBSP/30 ML)

2 1/2 TEASPOONS (5 G) CHOPPED ORGANIC LEMON
   ZEST (ABOUT ONE LEMON)

SALT

Prepare the tomatoes first; put them into a strainer while you ready the rest of the ingredients.

Slice the onion very thin. Mince the cilantro and the chili peppers.

Combine the tomatoes, onion, cilantro, peppers, and lime juice in a medium-size bowl. Add salt to taste and stir well. Cover and refrigerate for 1 hour. Transfer the mixture to a gravy boat before serving.

Pico de gallo *is often used to flavor tortillas or tacos. If you wish, you can also spread this salsa on toasted slices of rustic bread, serve it as a condiment for nachos, as a dip for raw vegetables, or as a dressing for salads or cold meats. This sauce is excellent fresh and can be safely stored (and still delicious) for up to three days. Pico de gallo (Spanish for "rooster's beak") is a staple in Mexican cuisine; it describes a variety of fresh sauces that feature the flavors of tomato, chili pepper, and onion punctuated with a burst of lime. Other ingredients such as avocado or radish may be included but they're not essential to create a perfect, refreshing and delicious pico de gallo.*

# HUMMUS WITH TAHINI

Difficulty of preparation: Medium - Degree of difficulty: Medium - Preparation time: 20 minutes - Cooking time: 3 hours - Soaking time: 8 hours

## INGREDIENTS FOR 4 PEOPLE

1 CUP (200 G) DRIED CHICKPEAS

2 CLOVES GARLIC

4 TBSP (60 G) TAHINI

2 DRIED AZERBAIJAN CHILLIES, CRUSHED AND
  SHREDDED

1 PINCH OF POWDERED CAYENNE CHILI PEPPER

JUICE OF 1 LEMON (ABOUT 1/4 CUP/60 ML)

1 TSP (3 G) SESAME SEEDS

2/3 CUP (10 G) FRESH PARSLEY,
  FINELY CHOPPED

2 TBSP (30 ML) EXTRA VIRGIN OLIVE OIL

SALT

Soak the chickpeas in cold water overnight or for at least 8 hours; drain, rinse, and drain again. Heat 4 cups of water to a simmer; keep hot until it's needed.

Peel and crush one of the cloves of garlic; cook it, along with the dried chili peppers, in the olive oil until golden brown, then add the chickpeas and season with a pinch of salt. Sauté for a few moments and pour in enough hot water to cover the chickpeas. Cover and cook over low heat for about 3 hours, adding more hot water if necessary. Drain, reserving the cooking liquid.

Blend the chickpeas with the remaining garlic, the tahini, the lemon juice and a pinch of salt. Pour in the broth little by little, stirring thoroughly, until the mixture is well blended and creamy. Transfer the hummus to a serving dish. Garnish with sesame seeds, parsley and chili powder to your liking and serve with vegetables, pita bread or pita chips.

*Hummus is an appetizer of Middle Eastern origins, and tahini, or sesame paste, is a key ingredient in any traditionally inspired hummus recipe. Lightly toasted white sesame seeds are crushed or pounded in a mortar to create a kind of flour that is infused with olive oil. Its texture resembles peanut butter, and in fact one of the common names for it is "sesame butter." In hummus, tahini is the essential balancing flavor for the chickpeas and gives this spread its rich, creamy consistency.*

# HARISSA SAUCE

## INGREDIENTS FOR 4 PEOPLE

5 CLOVES GARLIC

1 TBSP (6 G) CARVI SEEDS

5 SPRIGS FRESH CILANTRO

1 TBSP (2 G) GROUND CORIANDER

1 TBSP (1.5 G) DRIED MINT

10 RED AZERBAIJAN CHILI PEPPERS

10 HARISSA CHILI PEPPERS

EXTRA VIRGIN OLIVE OIL

SALT

Peel the garlic. Clean the chilies and the peppers and remove the stems. Cut them in half lengthwise and remove the white parts and seeds. Soak the chilies in cold water for about 1 hour, then drain and puree in a food processor. Add the coriander, mint, cumin, and cilantro and pulse to blend well. Drizzle in some oil gradually and continue processing until the mixture is thick and smooth. (The amount of oil – and time! – will vary.)

Serve harissa with olives and slices of white bread. To store for more than a few days, cover it with a layer of oil.

Harissa is a hot sauce from North Africa, where it's a main ingredient in the traditional cuisines, especially those of Tunisia. Its creamy texture, bright red color and deep, subtle fragrance are wonderfully appealing. It is a delightful spread on bread, topped with oil. Herbs can be added too, and it's an excellent appetizer. This spicy cream can also be mixed with salsas and sauces to flavor pasta, rice, kebabs and vegetables salads, either cooked or raw.

*The word* harissa *comes from an Arabic word meaning "to pound," and  the sauce may be made in a mortar, though it takes much longer this way. Prepared harissa is available in tubes, boxes, and cans at many specialty markets.*

# SMOKED PEPPER SAUCE

## INGREDIENTS FOR 4 PEOPLE

1/3 CUP (50 G) ONIONS

1 RED BELL PEPPER

4 SMOKED JALAPEÑO CHILI PEPPERS

2 TBSP (30 ML) EXTRA VIRGIN OLIVE OIL

To prepare this bell pepper and jalapeño pepper sauce, wash the bell pepper and cut into pieces; then peel and coarsely chop the onion and sauté these vegetables in oil.

Cook, covered, over medium heat for about 20 minutes, then add the chopped jalapeño chilies at the end. When the bell pepper and onion are well cooked, remove from heat and blend until the sauce is smooth and creamy.

The jalapeño pepper is often a spicy ingredient in Mexican cuisine. It can be used fresh, dried, pickled, and smoked. During the smoking process, the red color turns to black.

*The seeds and the innards of the jalapeño chili peppers can be removed, but if these remain the product is less refined. The jalapeño pepper has a thick, firm pulp that adds much to the flavor and texture of many dishes, from fajitas to burritos.*

# PILACCA (FRIED CHILI PEPPER SAUCE)

Difficulty of preparation: Easy - Degree of difficulty: Medium - Preparation time: 10 minutes - Resting time: 30 hours

MAKES 2 1/4 LB(1000 G)

| | |
|---|---|
| 1 YELLOW BELL PEPPER | 3/4 CUP (20 G) FRESH MINT |
| 1 RED BELL PEPPER | 1/3 CUP + 1 TBSP (10 G) FRESH PARSLEY |
| 1 FUEGUITOS CHILI PEPPER | 1/3 CUP + 1 TBSP (100 ML) WHITE VINEGAR |
| 2 STALKS CELERY | EXTRA VIRGIN OLIVE OIL |
| 1 CLOVE GARLIC | SALT |

Wash and dry the bell peppers, remove the stalks, white parts and seeds, then cut into small cubes (the smaller the better for the preparation). Lastly, transfer into a bowl.

Clean the chili pepper with a damp towel, remove the stalk and the seeds, then slice into rounds. Wash and dry the celery, remove the green leaves and any filaments, then chop finely and add it to the bell peppers. Then combine with sliced garlic, chili pepper, and salt and let stand in a cool place for a day, stirring from time to time. Pour the vegetables into a colander and let drain, then transfer them back into the bowl after it has been washed and dried.

Cover with vinegar and let stand for 3 hours. Finally, clean, wash and dry the herbs, then chop them. Drain the vegetables from the vinegar, flavor with herbs, place in jars and cover completely with oil. Close the jars and store the pilacca in a cool, dark place and let it sit for a few days before eating.

*This exquisite ingenuity hailing from Puglia, Italy, is the perfect condiment to transform slices of toasted bread into appetizing bruschetta; it can also be used to flavor sauces for pasta and vegetables. Preparing pilacca does not take any particular cooking skill, but rather a lot of patience to cut the vegetables into small pieces. The smaller the pieces, the better it becomes. Without a doubt, this colorful, joyful-looking preparation brings the flavor of sun and summer to the table!*

# FIG CHUTNEY

Difficulty of preparation: Medium · Degree of difficulty: Medium · Preparation time: 30 minutes · Cooking time: 15 minutes

## MAKES APPROXIMATELY 1 LB (500 G)

2/3 LBS (300 G) FRESH FIGS

1 MEDIUM SWEET ONION (ABOUT 3 1/2 OZ/100 G)

1 STALK LEMONGRASS

3 TBSP + 1 TSP (50 ML) BALSAMIC VINEGAR

1 OZ (30 G) CANE SUGAR

1 TSP (2 G) "FOUR SPICES" (A MIX OF GROUND
    CINNAMON, CLOVES, NUTMEG AND PEPPER)

2 INDIAN CHILI PEPPER

3/4 OZ (20 G) FRESH GINGER

1 TBSP (5 G) MUSTARD SEEDS

1 TBSP (5 G) CARDAMOM

1 TSP (2 G) GROUND CORIANDER

SALT

Gently wash the figs, peel them and cut half of them into small pieces. Wash and peel the onion, then slice it very thinly. Remove the cardamom from their pods. Wash the lemongrass and chop it finely. In a mortar, grind the chilies into powder. Peel and grate the ginger, then collect the pulp and the juice.

Pour the vinegar and sugar in a steel pot, boil for 3 to 4 minutes, then add all the figs and onions. Stir constantly and after a few more minutes add everything except the chili pepper.

Cook for about 10 minutes while stirring frequently; the mixture should thicken gently (adjust the heat if necessary so it does not burn). When the chutney thickens, add the chili pepper and season at will. In fact, it's right about now that you should really notice the chutney's splendid bouquet.

*This is a spicy sauce composed of fruit, spices and vegetables that is typical of Indian cuisine. It can be served with meat and rice or with cheese as a delightful appetizer or snack. There are many variations of chutney—mango, coconut, eggplant and tomato, to name a few— but the spices and the aromas remain unchanged in all of them. The "four spices" blend that's used in this preparation is a mix of cinnamon, cloves, nutmeg and pepper, all in powdered form. You can prepare it at home easily and season with chilies at will, as it is widely used in Middle Eastern cuisine. For preserves, put the hot chutney into sterilized jars, cap them, wrap them in cloths and boil for 20 minutes; let them cool, then remove them from the water and store a cool, dry, dark place. Once opened, the chutney will keep in the fridge for up to 4 days.*

# SPICY PICKLED TOMATOES

## MAKES 1 QUART (1 KILOGRAM)

2 1/4 LBS (1 KG) CHERRY TOMATOES

4 CLOVES GARLIC

1 1/2 OZ (40 G) FRESH GINGER

1 TSP (2 G) POWDERED ABBRACCIO CHILI PEPPERS

1 TSP (2 G) CUMIN

2 TSP (4 G) GROUND TURMERIC

3/4 CUP + 2 TBSP (200 ML) WHITE WINE VINEGAR

1/2 CUP (100 G) SUGAR

4 TBSP (60 ML) EXTRA VIRGIN OLIVE OIL

1 TSP (2 G) SEA SALT

3/4 CUP + 2 TBSP (200 ML) WATER

Prick the tomatoes with a needle (to keep them from bursting when the hot pickling liquid is poured over them), then divide them between the jars. Peel the garlic and slice very thin, about 1 millimeter thick. Peel the ginger with a vegetable peeler or paring knife, and cut into thin slices.

Heat the oil in a pan, then add the garlic, ginger, and chili powder. Stir with a wooden spoon, and after about 3 minutes, add the turmeric and cumin. Continue cooking for another minute, and stir in the vinegar, sugar, salt and water. Simmer for 4 to 5 minutes, stirring frequently.

Meanwhile, heat the jars in the oven at 480° F (250° C), or in boiling water for 5 minutes. Remove the jars from heat, place the tomatoes inside, push them gently to compact the mixture, but be careful not to squash them. Pour the herbed vinegar into the jars to completely cover the tomatoes. Close immediately and let cool. Keep the jars in the refrigerator and consume within 2 or 3 weeks.

*To best conserve this preparation, it is ideal to choose containers with caps that create a vacuum. This allows you to be sure that there is no air in the vessel and therefore no harmful toxins are formed and it can be stored for a few months. These delicious pickled spiced tomatoes are a wonderful side dish for meats and fish; they can also be used as the base for a delightful pasta sauce. Once the jars are opened, store in the fridge and use within 4 days.*

# TURKISH-STYLE EGGPLANT PRESERVES

*Difficulty of preparation: Easy - Degree of difficulty: Medium - Preparation time: 30 minutes - Cooking time: 5 minutes - Resting time: 4-5 hours*

## MAKES 1 QUART (1 KILOGRAM)

| | |
|---|---|
| 2 1/4 LBS (1 KG) EGGPLANT, ABOUT 2 MEDIUM | 2 SPRIGS OF THYME |
| 7 OZ (200 G) WALNUTS | 5 CLOVES GARLIC |
| 1 TBSP (5 G) POWDERED CAYENNE CHILI PEPPER | OLIVE OIL |
| 1 ACI SIVRI CHILI PEPPER | SALT (OPTIONAL) |

Bring salted water to boil in a stockpot. Wash the eggplant, remove the stem, and cut it lengthwise into slices that are about 2 millimeters thick. Cook the eggplant slices in the water for about 5 minutes, then drain them and let them dry on kitchen towels. Turn the slices several times, changing the towels as needed, until the slices have rendered all their liquid and are completely dry. This step is very important!

Make the "filling" for the eggplant. Peel and mince the garlic. Chop the walnuts roughly. Mix them both in a bowl with the cayenne pepper and salt to taste.

Sterilize the storage jars by placing them in boiling water for 5 minutes and remove them from the water only when ready to be filled. Use this spicy mixture to flavor the eggplant. Lay one slice of eggplant on a plate and spread a teaspoon of filling and the chopped aci sivri pepper along the middle. Roll the eggplant around the filling and place the rolls upright in the jars. Fit them snugly together but gently, so as not to tear them. Fill each jar to the brim with oil and drop in one sprig of thyme. Store in a cool place away from light.

*As with all canned goods, you must pay close attention that the ingredients do not ferment or deteriorate after the jar is closed, therefore closing the lid must form a vacuum and thus ensure the absence of air. The jar must then be kept in cool and dry place. This specialty from Turkey is magnificent when finely chopped and used to prepare sauces for pastas, rice and meat.*

# PICKLED EGGPLANT

**MAKES 1 QUART (1 KILOGRAM)**

2 1/4 LBS (1 KG) EGGPLANT, ABOUT 2 MEDIUM

6 RED ACROBATA CHILI PEPPERS

10 CLOVES GARLIC

EXTRA VIRGIN OLIVE OIL

1 OZ (20 G) FRESH OREGANO

1/3 CUP (30 G) FENNEL SEEDS

3/4 CUP + 2 TBSP (200 ML) WHITE VINEGAR

SEA SALT

Wash and dice the eggplant. To draw the moisture out of the eggplant, sprinkle it with salt and let the liquid drain for 5 minutes. Wash and pat dry. Put the cubes in a container, add the vinegar, cover the container and leave in a cool, dry place for 2 days.

Peel the garlic and wash the peppers. Pour the eggplant into a colander and squeeze it well. Divide between two sterilized jars and top with a pinch of salt, half the oregano, half the fennel seeds, 5 garlic cloves and 3 chili peppers per jar. Mash the contents well, then fill to the brim with oil and seal the lid tightly. Store preserves in a cool, dry, dark place; once opened, the relish will keep for a week in the fridge.

To sterilize the jars, wrap them in cloths, place in a saucepan, cover with water and boil for about 30 minutes, then let cool.

*This originally Calabrian preserve ideally accompanies grilled meats and fish. It's great as an appetizer alongside other vegetables, either fresh or pickled. This perfect appetizer tantalizes the senses with the spicy and acidic aroma contained within the rich pieces of eggplant.*

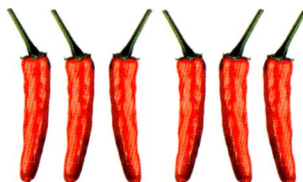

# DESSERTS

When it comes to desserts, the most comforting and sinful dishes of any meal, the chili pepper can be a secret weapon, provided it's handled with care. The goal is to find that perfect sweet-spicy balance, a harmony that makes dishes intriguing and tasty. We are not the first to mix chocolate and chili pepper, capsicum and cream. The Aztecs (about 8000 years ago!), after all, were already experimenting with the combination, matching the energy of one with the tantalizing appeal of the other. Much later, pharmacist Wilbur Scoville, developed a method to measure the heat level of a chili pepper, making it more convenient to work with them.

There were also six degrees established by the Aztecs: coco, hot; cocpatic, very hot; cocopetz-patic, very, very hot; cocopetztic, brilliant hot; cocpetzquauitl, extremely hot; and cocpalatic, runaway hot. Running away, however, won't save mucous membranes from powerful peppers. Instead, it helps to pair the very spiciest peppers with foods like milk or cream. This is why desserts, which often involve dairy products, are a perfect outlet for the chili pepper.

In Modica, Sicily, chocolate is a specialty all its own, drawing inspiration from the original recipes of South America by mixing the idealino or habanero to obtain an aromatic compound, one that is very flirty and exciting. For the powerful Modica chocolate cake, meanwhile, we recommend a pairing with spiced wine or rum.

Gingerbread is an unexpected and utterly delightful pairing for super-hot habaneros. The trick is to keep your level of heat tolerance in mind, remembering that this pepper is considered cocopalatic!

For something a bit less spicy, you have the two-jam tart, the orange blending wonderfully with the delicato pepper, resulting in a good sweet-spicy balance. This delicious dessert is perfect not only at the end of a meal, but also for breakfast, making sure you start the day with energy and focus!

And for a special moment during the day? An original and very aromatic preparation can be achieved by combining certain ingredients, including ricotta, rum and vanilla, in chocolate. Mixed with the chili de onza, the dolcevita the agata, the result is divine.

For a moment of pure pleasure at the end of a meal, a few spoonfuls of spiced chocolate, enriched by the strong abbraccio, will do the trick. The soft, cozy cream is perfect for a momentary break, an escape from daily tasks, particularly when you couple it with a shot of whiskey.

Desserts, of course, are also suitable as gifts, so why not prepare spiced sweets as an original present? With minimum kitchen skills, you can prepare desserts in colored paper; desserts that, if you know the recipient's tastes, can have the perfect amount of capsicum and heat. In this case, the choice will fall on the Brazilian cheiro and daddy peppers, the first only mildly spicy and aromatic, the second medium strong. Both, however, are well balanced with other ingredients.

On a special day like Valentine's Day, desserts are essential, and the Spicy Saint Valentine recipe, prepared with the fatalii and fueguitos peppers, has what it takes to get the heart racing. Some do say that the chili pepper is something of an aphrodisiac. While this is just hearsay, one thing is certain: The right dessert can spice up just about any evening, even if only for a moment or two!

# RED HABANERO QUINCE

Difficulty of preparation: Easy - Difficulty of cooking: Easy - Preparation time: 19 minutes - Cooking time: 30 minutes

## INGREDIENTS FOR 2 PEOPLE

1 QUINCE

1 GLASS OF RED WINE

1 3/4 OZ (50 G) SUGAR CANE

HALF A FRESH HABANERO CHILI PEPPER

1 DRIED HABANERO CHILI PEPPER, CHOPPED

1 OZ (30 G) OF DARK CHOCOLATE

1 TBSP (9 G) OF ALMOND FLAKES

Wash the quince, peel and cut into slices about half a centimeter thick. Using enough water to cover the contents, boil the quince slices in a saucepan with the half fresh habanero pepper (cut into 2 parts), sugar cane and half the red wine.

Cook over low heat for 20 to 25 minutes, so that the slices of quince are soft, and gradually add the remaining wine. Keep covered so that the cooking liquids do not evaporate, and if you have to add more hot water, do so little by little. When the slices are of the desired consistency, remove from heat, let cool and drain on a wooden board.

Arrange the slices of quince on a serving dish. Grate the chocolate and then melt it in a *bain marie*, adding some crushed red pepper. Stir regularly to mix the flavors and let cook until a smooth and creamy fudge develops. Using a spoon, distribute small amounts of chocolate over the quince slices, forming irregular lines and decorative designs. Finish with the sliced almonds and serve.

*Red wine quince is a simple and natural dessert that is fragrant and decidedly aromatic. It perfectly balances and combines the spice of the habanero and the sweetness of the melted chocolate. This recipe is particularly suitable for the cold season. Red wine reduced from the cooking blends beautifully with other ingredients. Easy to prepare, but impressive in its beauty and flavor, it is a perfect dessert for lunch or a formal dinner. A glass of sweet red wine is the perfect complement to this dessert.*

# STRAWBERRIES
# WITH SPICY CHOCOLATE

## INGREDIENTS FOR 2 PEOPLE

10 FRESH STRAWBERRIES
2 OZ (60 G) DARK CHOCOLATE
1/2 TSP (1 G) POWDERED HABANERO

Thoroughly wash the strawberries, but don't remove the stems, which will serve for dipping the strawberries. Grate the chocolate and melt it in a *bain marie* stirring regularly. Add the chili pepper, measuring the amount to suit your taste for spice.

When the chocolate has melted, stir it with a small whisk or a wooden spatula, dipping the strawberries one at a time and placing them on a plate or a sheet of baking paper. When chocolate cools, it will harden. Store them in a cool place until serving time.

Just before serving, gently pull the strawberries off the paper and arrange them on individual dishes according to your taste and imagination. This dessert can be served by bringing the melted dark chocolate to the table, keeping its little pot warm with a small flame or a candle. You and your guests can then dip the strawberries in the melted chocolate by holding on to the stem or with the help of skewers.

*Strawberries covered with spicy chocolate are a delicious and intriguing dessert, perfect for a special evening, teasing the senses with the wonderful contrast between the crunchy, melted chocolate and fresh, juicy strawberries. It is a perfect dessert that preserves the natural bouquet of the fruit, the chili peppers and the chocolate...one that seems designed for Valentine's Day! Serve the chocolate covered strawberries with a glass of rum or good quality vodka.*

# SPICY SAINT VALENTINE!

## INGREDIENTS FOR 2 PEOPLE

3 1/2 OZ (100 G) CREAM CHEESE

2 3/4 OZ (80 G) DARK CHOCOLATE

3 TBSP + 1 TSP (40 G) ICING SUGAR

1 TBSP (15 ML) AMARETTO LIQUEUR

1/3 OZ (10 G) SLICED ALMONDS

1 POWDERED FATALII CHILI PEPPER

2 FRESH FUEGUITOS CHILI PEPPERS
   FOR DECORATION

Grate the chocolate and melt it in a *bain marie*, add the habanero chili powder, according to your taste. The amount of chili used varies, and it is particularly suitable for the preparation of highly aromatic desserts involving habanero or amachito peppers. Spread 6 generous tablespoons of melted chocolate on a baking tray lined with greaseproof paper (e.g. baking or wax paper) in a thin layer to make the sheet. Use a mold to create the shape of the heart. Make 6 hearts and let harden in the fridge.

In the meantime, prepare the mousse. For the white part: mix half the cheese with the amaretto and just over half the powdered sugar. Blend the ingredients until the mixture is smooth, light and homogenous. Transfer to a pastry bag (with a medium sized tip) and leave in the fridge until ready to use. Prepare the chocolate mousse by mixing the remaining cheese with the rest of the powdered sugar and 2 tablespoons of the melted chocolate/chili mixture. Mix with an electric mixer until you have a creamy compound with the desired consistency. Transfer to a pastry bag with a medium sized nozzle.

To prepare for serving, arrange the dessert directly on individual dishes, starting with a dark chocolate heart as a base; a layer of chocolate mousse; a sheet of chocolate; the cream cheese; and finish with another chocolate sheet. Replace in the fridge. Immediately before serving, sprinkle with the chopped almonds and decorate with a fresh chili pepper cut into 2 parts.

*This two mousse dessert is sweet and sophisticated, an ideal dish to excite the senses and end a special meal (perhaps a Valentine's day dinner) on a sweet and spicy note. Patience is required to make this dessert, so don't be afraid to make mistakes when preparing the dark chocolate sheets. If they are not immediately workable, you can always re-create them (and there may not be a more delicious mistake!) until you perfect them.*

# SPICED PEARLS

## INGREDIENTS FOR 4 PEOPLE

8 3/4 OZ (250 G) FRESH SHEEP'S MILK RICOTTA

3 1/2 OZ (100 G) 70% DARK CHOCOLATE

1/2 TSP (1 G) CHILI DE ONZA PEPPER POWDER

3 TBSP + 1 TSP (40 G) SUGAR

1/3 CUP + 1 TBSP (50 G) COCONUT FLOUR

1 VANILLA POD

1 TBSP (15 ML) DARK RUM

Break up the chocolate and melt it in a *bain marie*, stirring regularly. Sieve the ricotta and stir in the chili (if you're accustomed to spice, if not, use just a little bit at a time to find a level you're comfortable with). Stir with a whisk, add the sugar, the seeds of the vanilla pod and rum.

Knead the ingredients until you have made a well-combined and creamy compound. Slowly pour the melted chocolate, half of the coconut flour and quickly stir the ingredients before the mixture hardens. Let rest in the fridge for 30 minutes so that the chocolate dough hardens so that you can then knead the pearls.

Pour the flour and coconut into a bowl, take the dough from the refrigerator, and with a spoon, take enough (depending on the desired size) to make a ball. Knead with your hands to give it a spherical shape and dip the pearl in coconut. Press the mixture lightly to compact it and put it on a flat plane. Continue this way until you finish the ingredients and then let the chocolate stand in the refrigerator for 30 minutes. At serving time transfer the pearls to a serving dish.

*These elegant pearls, which incorporate the exotic flavors of tropical countries, enveloping vanilla, sweet coconut, spicy chili, strong and aromatic rum, all bound by chocolate (and delivered in a simple and beautiful sphere), seem to come from the hands great pastry chefs. Whether they are served as a break between courses, during a nice romantic cuddle, or at the end of the meal, the ingredients, which leave lingering flavors on your palate, conjure up far away countries (even if the ingredients are all easily found). A sip of aged rum is the liquor that best helps you appreciate these chocolate pearls.*

# SPICY CHOCOLATE SAUCE

Difficulty of preparation: Easy - Difficulty of cooking: Easy - Preparation time: 10 minutes - Cooking time: 10 minutes - Resting time: 4 hours

## INGREDIENTS FOR 4 PEOPLE

3 1/3 OZ (100 ML) MILK
3 1/3 OZ (100 ML) WHIPPED CREAM
3 1/2 OZ (100 G) 70% DARK CHOCOLATE
1 TBSP + 1 TSP (20 G) SUGAR
2 ABBRACCIO CHILI PEPPERS
1 CINNAMON STICK
1 CLOVE

Pour the milk into a saucepan, bring to a boil then turn off, remove from heat and crumble in the cinnamon, 1 pepper and clove. Let stand at room temperature for 3 to 4 hours and then filter.

Break up and chop the chocolate into small pieces with the aid of a knife on a cutting board. Pour flavored milk into a pot, place it on the stove over low heat, add the chocolate, pour the cream and let it "warm" (not boil) until the chocolate melts and amalgams perfectly with the other ingredients. Stir constantly and when the cream seems to increase slightly in volume, remove from heat and pour into a container that you will use to serve the sauce, as it will thicken once cooled and become impossible to pour.

Decorate the top with crumbled chili pepper. Serve warm or at room temperature. You can pair the sauce with biscuits or bread sticks, or as an ice cream topping. For the more daring, you can even pair the sauce with cream cheese.

*The cold months are most suitable for this sauce, which thanks to the chili peppers, will keep you warm toasty on the inside! Spicy chocolate sauce is an intriguing, aromatic cream worthy of special occasions or when trying to relax. Alternating the rich flavor of the spices with a dry hard liquor like whiskey is a good idea, providing a seductive combination that brings out the best in both the dessert and the drink.*

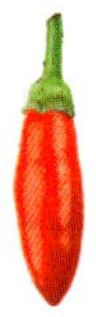

# HOT CHOCOLATE TARTS

## INGREDIENTS FOR 4 PEOPLE

7 OZ (200 G) READY-MADE PUFF PASTRY

3 1/2 OZ (100 G) CHOCOLATE

1 HABANERO CHILI PEPPER (POWDERED)

1 FRESH SALAMANDRA CHILI PEPPER

1 EGG

1/3 CUP (60 G) SUGAR

2 SHEETS OF GELATIN (6 G)

3 1/3 OZ (100 ML) WHIPPING CREAM

BUTTER FOR THE MOLDS

Preheat the oven to 350° F (180° C). Unroll the pastry onto a lightly floured surface, divide into 4 parts and with a pastry ring, make 4 discs with a diameter of about 5 1/2 inches (14 centimeters). Spread a little butter on 4 round baking pans (for individual serving), place the dough and settle it with your hands, pierce with a fork and bake for about 10 minutes, then remove and let cool at room temperature.

Whip the cream with a whisk and keep in refrigerator until ready to use. Break up the chocolate and melt it in a bain marie; soften gelatin in cold water, drain and incorporate the chocolate when hot, stir in the chili powder (according to your taste). Mix the ingredients until the gelatin is fully incorporated into the chocolate. In a large bowl, beat the egg with the sugar and work until soft and creamy.

Stir in the chili pepper to the chocolate cream, working the ingredients with a whisk, then add the cream, stirring gently with a wooden spatula so the cream does not break apart. Transfer the cream into a pastry bag and fill the tart crust. Leave in the refrigerator until ready to serve. Remove the tarts from the refrigerator at least 10 minutes before serving, decorate with red pepper slices cut at the time of serving.

*With mousse tarts, it's all about the contrasts: crunchy and soft, sweet and spicy, light and dark, all of which highlighted by the simple beauty and the fragrant scent. A tip to ensure an easy preparation: you can purchase ready made pastry "pockets" which can help streamline the work. The tarts are perfect for a snack or a tasty breakfast (during the day, try it with a cup of tea), however it can also work well with a glass of dessert wine at the end of an evening meal.*

# MODICA CHOCOLATE CAKE

## INGREDIENTS FOR 6 PEOPLE

1/4 LBS (110 G) DARK CHOCOLATE FLAVORED WITH
   CHILI PEPPER (E.G., MODICA CHOCOLATE)
1/2 CUP (110 G) CANE SUGAR
3 1/3 OZ (100 ML) DARK RUM
1 STICK UNSALTED BUTTER
3 EGGS
1/2 CUP (60 G) BISCUITS

1/2 CUP (60 G) WHITE FLOUR
1 PACKET OF BAKING POWDER
SALT
*TO DECORATE:*
2 CUPS (400 G) WHIPPED CREAM
1 IDEALINO CHILI PEPPER

Preheat the oven to 350° F (180° C) and line a cake pan with parchment paper. Moisten it slightly to help it mold to the pan. Separate the yolks from the whites and whip the whites until they start to stiffen (help them out with a pinch of salt!). Chop the chocolate, transfer to a bowl and then melt it in a bain marie. Meanwhile, work the butter with the sugar with a whisk until it is fluffy but dense, incorporate the egg yolks one at a time, then the melted chocolate and the rum. Stir until creamy and smooth and without lumps.

Crumble the biscuits finely, add them to the other ingredients in the bowl. Sift the flour, baking powder, mix well and when you get a smooth mixture, very gently fold in the egg whites with a wooden spoon.

Then pour the mixture into the parchment-lined pan, level and bake for 30 minutes. Remove from the oven, allow to cool for 10 minutes. Shortly before serving, gently remove the baking paper to avoid damaging the cake, place the cake on a glass cake holder and decorate with slices of fresh chili cut into rings. Serve with whipped cream.

*For the preparation of this cake you can use already flavored chocolate, such as that from Modica, Sicily, which has a classic, almost rustic quality (homemade characteristics that suit this cake, which is inspired by South American recipes). Alternatively, you can combine good chocolate with chili peppers like the habanero, and spicy amachito. Serve the cake with an aromatic white wine or agricultural rum.*

# HABANERO GINGERBREAD

*Difficulty of preparation: Medium - Difficulty of cooking: Easy - Preparation time: 20 minutes - Cooking time: 30-40 minutes - Resting time: 2 hours*

## INGREDIENTS FOR 4 PEOPLE

2 3/4 CUP + 1 TBSP (350 G) FLOUR

HALF A SACHET OF YEAST

250 G OF HONEY

1/2 CUP + 2 TBSP (125 G) SUGAR

2 EGGS

1 SMALL LEMON

1 CLOVE

4 1/2 OZ (125 G) SHELLED ALMONDS

1 POWDERED HABANERO CHILI PEPPER

1/2 TSP (1 G) OF CINNAMON

3 TBSP (45 ML) EXTRA VIRGIN OLIVE

SALT AND PEPPERCORNS

Melt the honey in a saucepan with the sugar and extra virgin olive oil, mixing thoroughly until a you have an homogeneous and fluid syrup. Crush the chili in a mortar.

Wash and grate the lemon zest; ground the cloves in a blender or mortar. Sift the flour into a large bowl that can hold all the ingredients and add the baking powder, almonds, ground pepper, powdered clove, a pinch of salt, cinnamon and half a gram of powdered chili. (The amount of peppers varies depending on your enjoyment of spice!). Knead the ingredients, incorporating the eggs one at a time, finally add the honey and the lemon zest.

Leave the dough covered with a cloth in a cool and dark place for at least 2 hours. Preheat the oven at 390° F (200° C), cover a rectangular pan with parchment paper. Transfer the dough by pressing down lightly at the edges, bake for 30 to 40 minutes, then remove from oven and shape (when the gingerbread is room temperature). Remove the wax paper and gently cut the dessert into slices about 1 cm thick.

*Gingerbread is a rich, tasty and fragrant cake. Traditionally, it is prepared at Christmas time (in Italy, and in particular in Umbria, it is a symbol of prosperity). At one time, gingerbread was reserved for important people and every family guarded a special recipe with a secret ingredient that only the baker was aware of. A spice-rich bread by name, this dessert (once rare and hard to find) is fragrant, tasty and nutritious. This cake can be stored for long periods and is suitable for accompanying sauces, desserts, chocolate. It can also be dipped in a red wine.*

# SPICY STRUDEL

## INGREDIENTS FOR 4 PEOPLE

14 OZ (400 G) READY-MADE RECTANGULAR
   PUFF PASTRY
3 MEDIUM-SIZED RIPE PEARS
3 1/2 OZ (100 G) DARK CHOCOLATE BLOCKS OR CHIPS
2 OZ (60 G) ALMONDS

1 TSP (2 G) GROUND CINNAMON HARISSA
   CHILI POWDER TO TASTE
BUTTER
1 TBSP + 2 TSP (20 G) ICING SUGAR

Wash and peel the pears, remove the cores and cut into small cubes. Melt the butter in a non-stick frying pan and add the chunks fruit. Sprinkle with cinnamon powder and hot pepper, stir, taste and adjust the seasoning to your taste. Continue cooking for about 5 minutes on medium-high heat, until the water has evaporated, then remove from heat and let cool.

Meanwhile, chop the almonds and the dark chocolate into flakes (if desired you can also use chocolate chips). Coat a rectangular baking sheet with wax paper, unroll the dough, divide into 4 rectangles, fill them with fruit, almonds and chocolate. Place the stuffing in the middle, leaving the edges free so that you can easily close the strudels. Cover, making sure the edges stick together well, thus creating 4 rectangular bundles. With a knife, make small cuts at the top of the strudels and place on the wax paper.

Preheat the oven to 390° F (200° C) and bake the strudel for about 15 to 20 minutes. The dessert is cooked when the pastry has lightly puffed and is golden in color (hint: your kitchen will have been flooded with an irresistibly fragrant aroma). Remove from the oven and let them cool. Before serving, sprinkle powdered sugar on top.

*This recipe has endless delicious variations both sweet and savory. It's no surprise that it is made around the world. Strudel, derived from the German word for "whirlpool", is perfect anytime of the day, from breakfast to the end of a late-night meal. Excellent with a glass of sweet white wine.*

# ORANGE AND FUEGUITOS COOKIES

## INGREDIENTS FOR 4 PEOPLE

1/2 STICK + 2 TBSP (100 G) BUTTER

3/4 CUP + 1 TBSP (100 G) ICING SUGAR

1 1/4 CUP (150 G) FLOUR

1/2 TSP (1 1/3 G) DRIED, CRUSHED FUEGUITOS CHILI PEPPER

1/2 TSP (1 1/3 G) GROUND CINNAMON

1 TSP (5 ML) VANILLA EXTRACT

ZEST AND JUICE OF 1 ORGANIC ORANGE

1 1/2 OZ (40 G) DARK CHOCOLATE

HALF A SACHET OF YEAST

Wash the orange, grate the rind, avoiding the white part, then cut it in half and squeeze out the juice. Put the butter in a bowl and melt it in a bain marie; when it is melted, stir in the powdered sugar with a whisk until creamy. Continue stirring and sift in the flour, then add the yeast, cinnamon, orange peel (leaving a spoonful aside) and ground chili. Then combine with 2 tablespoons of orange juice and work until you have a homogeneous mixture.

Preheat the oven to 390° F (200° C). Coat a rectangular pan with parchment paper. Break up the chocolate, add it to the other ingredients and stir with a whisk or wooden spoon until it becomes a smooth paste. Then transferred to a wood or marble surface and work it until you have a cylinder with a diameter of roughly 2 inches (5 centimeters). Cut into slices, arrange them on baking sheet and bake.

Bake the cookies for about 10 minutes, or until they take on a nice golden color. Then remove from oven, let cool and then transfer the cookies into a serving dish and garnish with the remaining orange peel.

*Orange and amachito chili chocolate cookies are a simple, easy to prepare dessert that can be enjoyed for up to a week. The different flavors blend perfectly with each other and achieve a true harmony of tastes and scents. It's a spiced dessert that is perfect as an exotic snack, and great to munch on without spoiling your dinner! Great dipped in tea for breakfast (particularly with a hint of orange marmalade), it can also be dipped in a wonderful glass of white wine.*

# CHILI AND LEMON PUDDING

## INGREDIENTS FOR 4 PEOPLE

13.50 FL. OZ (400 ML) OF MILK

2 TBSP (30 ML) HONEY

2 EGGS

1/3 CUP + 1 TBSP (50 G) 00 WHITE FLOUR

5 1/2 TSP (15 G) POTATO STARCH

1/3 OZ (10 G) OF VANILLA

HALF A SACHET OF YEAST

1/4 CUP (50 G) GRANULATED SUGAR

DRY GROUND CAMARENA CHILI PEPPER

2 ORGANIC LEMONS

1 BUNCH OF MINT

Wash 1 lemon, zest it, and juice it. Combine half the juice with half the sugar in a saucepan on medium heat, stirring constantly so that it lightly caramelizes. As soon as the mixture thickens and begins to bubble, pour into 4 individual serving molds, preferably made out of silicone.

Beat the eggs lightly with a fork in a large bowl. Sift the flour and potato starch, add the yeast. Add the half the lemon zest and the remaining juice, the caramelized sugar, milk, honey, eggs and pepper (to taste). Work the ingredients with an electric mixer until the mixture is smooth and transfer it into 4 individual containers.

Preheat the oven to 350° F (180° C) and bake the puddings in a *bain marie* for about 20 to 25 minutes, checking that they have thickened; if not, continue cooking for another 5 minutes. Remove from oven and let cool. Before serving, wash the remaining lemon and slice it. Wash the mint. At serving time, garnish with slices of lemon, lemon peel and mint leaves.

*Lemon chili pudding is a delicious, light and fresh-tasting dessert. The beauty of the recipe is that you can control the amount of chili pepper used, accentuating or reducing the contrasting between the aromatic sweetness of the dish and the heat of the amachito. Moderation, however, is always recommended. Because of its soft and delicate features, this pudding recipe is a perfect dessert to end a fish meal. For followers of Bacchus, a light, fresh white wine is recommended, while teetotalers can enjoy a glass of well-chilled lemonade.*

# CHOCOLATE CHILI HEARTS

Difficulty of preparation: Difficult - Difficulty of cooking: Medium - Preparation time: 20 minutes - Cooking time: 15 minutes - Resting time: 3 hours

## INGREDIENTS FOR 4 PEOPLE

1/3 CUP + 1 TBSP (50 G) FLOUR

7 OZ (200 G) OF DARK CHOCOLATE

3/4 CUP + 1 TBSP (160 G) SUGAR

3/4 CUP (160 G) BUTTER

4 EGGS

1 HABANERO CHILI PEPPER POWDER

4 FRESH SALAMANDRA CHILI PEPPERS

1 PINCH OF SALT

Melt the chocolate in a *bain marie* with the butter and stir in the chili powder to your liking – but be considerate of your guests' liking, too! Add sugar and continue stirring to mix the ingredients together. Remove the mixture from heat and let cool, stirring regularly. Meanwhile, separate the yolks from the egg whites and work the latter with whisk and a pinch of salt to stiffen them.

Combine the egg yolks with the melted chocolate one at a time, then sift in the flour. Finally with the aid of a wooden spatula, stir in the egg whites and work until they stiffen. Cover 4 individual serving molds with parchment paper, fill them 2/3 of the way with the mixture and then put them in the freezer for 3 hours. This step is essential to ensure that the hearts maintain their molten centers even when cooked.

Just before bringing to the table, preheat the oven to 390° F (200° C), remove the cakes from the freezer, bake and cook until they puff up (about 8 to 10 minutes), then remove, let cool 5 minutes, and plate. Garnish with fresh chili peppers.

*Chocolate hearts are a dessert with an enveloping sweetness, a pleasant dash of spice, and a unique consistency (which can be attributed to time in the freezer before cooking). This recipe is inspired by cakes in Piedmont (northern Italy), and was said to be a favorite of the Savoy and Camillo Benso, the Count of Cavour. Crisp on the outside and gooey in its center, these chocolate hearts are irresistible desserts that make a perfect end to a great meal. A fresh and light moscato wine is a great accompaniment.*

# CHILI APPLE PIE

## INGREDIENTS FOR 4 PEOPLE

*FOR THE PASTRY:*
1 2/3 CUPS (200 G) FLOUR
1/4 CUP (50 G) GRANULATED SUGAR
2/3 CUP (150 G) BUTTER
1 EGG YOLK
3 TBSP COLD WATER
A PINCH OF SALT

*FOR THE FILLING:*
12 1/3 OZ (350 G) GOLDEN APPLES
1/4 CUP (50 G) CANE SUGAR
1 3/4 OZ (50 G) ALMONDS
ZEST FROM 1 ORGANIC ORANGE
1/2 TBSP (4 G) POTATO STARCH
1 DRIED DADDY CHILI PEPPER, GROUND
1/2 TSP (1 1/3 G) GROUND CINNAMON

Whisk the egg yolk with water and half the sugar. Cut the butter into small pieces and let it soften at room temperature. Measure the flour, butter and salt onto a work surface. Knead the ingredients until you have large chickpea-like crumbs, then add the beaten egg yolk and knead quickly. Beat the dough several times on the work surface and make a ball, repeating the operation several times until you have a smooth dough. Wrap in plastic and let rest in the refrigerator for 30 minutes.

Meanwhile prepare the filling: Coarsely chop half the almonds and put all the almonds into a bowl; cut the orange zest into small pieces and add it to the almonds. Wash the apples, peel them, cut them into slices and mix them with the almonds. Mix ingredients with half the cane sugar, the potato starch, the cinnamon and a pinch of red chili pepper (according to your taste). Preheat the oven to 350° F (180° C). Line a baking sheet with parchment paper. Spread the dough on a floured board, and make a disk shape that is larger than pan, with a thickness of about 3 millimeters. Place the pastry into the pan, spread the filling, cover with the edges of the pastry, brush with water and distribute the sugar on top.

Bake for 35 to 40 minutes until the pastry is golden brown. Then remove from the oven, letting it cool and form in the air. Remove the paper and put the cake on a serving plate. Serve at room temperature or at least several minutes after removing it from a hot oven.

*This cake is a variation of the classic American apple pie: a cake that uses very little sugar and brings out the tantalizing and fragrant aroma of the pepper-flavored filling. Try it with a sweet or flavored white wine or with aged cognac.*

# HAZELNUT CHILI CAKES

## INGREDIENTS FOR 4 PEOPLE

3 1/2 OZ (100 G) SHELLED HAZELNUTS

1/2 CUP (100 G) UNREFINED CANE SUGAR

1/2 STICK + 2 TBSP (100 G) BUTTER

1 1/4 CUP (150 G) 00 WHITE FLOUR

1 3/4 OZ (50 G) DARK CHOCOLATE

2 DROPS OF VANILLA ESSENCE

FATALII CHILI POWDER

8 FRESH ALFIERE CHILI PEPPERS FOR DECORATION

Cut the butter into small pieces and let it soften for ten minutes at room temperature. Meanwhile, grate the dark chocolate. Toast the hazelnuts in the oven at 350° F (180° C) for 10 minutes, then remove, leaving the oven on—it will need to be hot for the cakes! Chop the hazelnuts finely and put them in a bowl. Add sugar, vanilla essence and a pinch of pepper (or more, depending on your tastes).

Incorporate the butter and other ingredients, stir and add the chocolate. With a wooden spoon, combine all the ingredients until creamy, well mixed and smooth. Cover 8 small containers with a diameter of about 4 to 5 inches with parchment paper (to make working with the paper easier, moisten and squeeze it into place. The moisture will allow it to stick more easily).

Shape into balls that can fit in the molds (they should not fill more than half of the container). Arrange on a baking tray and bake for 15 to 20 minutes. Then take them out and let them cool at room temperature. Just before serving, transfer the cakes to a serving dish. Garnish with fresh chili pepper and bring to the table.

*These spicy hot cakes can be conserved for a few days. Store them in a cool, dry place and pop them in the oven at 390 degrees F to regain a bit of vitality and freshness. It's a simple dessert, perfect to dip in sweet white wine. In Piedmont, Italy, where the hazelnut reigns supreme, cookies and cakes are served with moscato d'Asti, a sweet sparkling white wine with a low alcohol content.*

# SPICED CANDY

## INGREDIENTS FOR 4 PEOPLE

6 3/4 OZ (200 ML) FRESH CREAM

3/4 LBS (120 G) DARK CHOCOLATE

1 CUP (200 G) SUGAR

1 TBSP (15 G) HONEY

1 CINNAMON STICK

1 DRIED CHEIRO CHILI PEPPER

COLORED PAPER AND ALUMINUM FOIL

Break up the chocolate and melt it over low heat in a bain marie. Meanwhile, flavor the cream by heating it with cinnamon and crumbled chili. Bring to a boil, turn off and filter. Pour 3 tablespoons of sugar into a saucepan - spoonful after spoonful - and let it caramelize over a gentle heat. When finished, slowly pour the cream and honey and stir until the ingredients are well combined. Remove from heat.

Pour half the chocolate into the mixture, stirring to combine the ingredients. Put on the stove and bring to a temperature of 230° F (110° C) – about 6 to 7 minutes on medium heat. It's ready if a tablespoon of the mixture thickens quickly when poured onto a marble slab. When it has reached temperature, remove from heat, add remaining ingredients, stir and pour into a rectangular mold and let thicken.

When it comes time to package the cookies, cut the compound into pieces and place the pieces in aluminum foil and then wrap colored paper. Serve at room temperature. This dessert is conserved during cold months, as at that time of year, the cookies do not even need to be stored in the fridge. In contrast, you can wrap the cookies a little at a time and keep the mixture stored and readied in the refrigerator.

*The habit of associating chili peppers with chocolate dates back to pre-Columbian times and this exotic combination continues to win fans! Outside of South America, Modica, Italy, is one of the few places in the West that is keeping this tradition alive. The cheiro chili pepper is particularly aromatic and mildly spicy, allowing for errors of quantity. It is thus recommended for those just getting used to spicy foods! This recipe works especially well with a sweet passito from Pantelleria (Italy).*

# TWO-JAM TART

## INGREDIENTS FOR 8 PEOPLE

*FOR THE DOUGH:*
2 1/3 CUPS + 1 TBSP (300 G) FLOUR
2/3 CUP (150 G) BUTTER
3/4 CUP (150 G) SUGAR
2 EGG YOLKS AND 1 WHOLE EGG
1 PACKET OF YEAST
ZEST OF 1 LEMON

*FOR THE FILLING:*
1/2 CUP (150 G) ORANGE MARMALADE
1/3 CUP (100 G) DELICATO CHILI PEPPER JAM
3 1/2 OZ (100 G) BLANCHED ALMONDS
COOKING SPRAY OR BUTTER FOR GREASING THE PAN
*FOR THE DELICATO CHILI PEPPER JAM:*
10 1/2 OZ (300 G) DELICATO CHILI PEPPERS
(100 G) CANE SUGAR

First, prepare the jam. Remove the stalk or stem, seeds, and placenta (inner ribbing) from the chili peppers. Then cut the chili peppers into pieces and cook uncovered along with the sugar over low heat for about an hour, stirring regularly. The peppers should melt almost completely and thicken because of the sugar. When cooking is done, the mixture should be reduced by half. Remove from the heat and let cool to room temperature. Wash the lemon and grate the peel. Cut the butter into small pieces and let it soften at room temperature. Pour the flour onto a work surface, add the sugar, egg yolks and lemon peel and gradually stir the butter and yeast. The pastry should not be heated and therefore do not knead, simply combine the ingredients, which will be held together with the butter. When the dough thickens up, wrap in plastic wrap and let rest in refrigerator for 30 minutes.

Preheat the oven to 350° F (180° C). Finely chop the almonds with a mixer or a mortar. Divide the dough into 2 portions, one slightly larger for the base and a smaller one for the cover. Thin out the first one with a rolling pin on a lightly floured surface. Butter the sides and bottom of a round baking pan, place the dough, making sure it adheres well.

Spread the marmalade, overlay red pepper, then distribute the almonds. With the dough, make a pastry roughly half a centimeter thick, with a knife make strips and by overlaying jam, create a grid by placing rows, horizontally and diagonally. Bake for about 30 minutes, then remove from the oven, allow to cool and gently form. Serve at room temperature accompanied with chili jam.

*The two-jam tart, like all cakes, is a triumph of fragrant aroma, an apparently simple treat that nevertheless requires a harmony of tastes and a perfect balance of ingredients. The crispness of the crust goes beautifully with the soft, slightly bitter flavor of the orange marmalade and spicy chili. It's a perfect dessert to end a meal involving meat or cheese. Excellent with a glass of robust red wine.*

# ALPHABETICAL INDEX OF RECIPES

# ALPHABETICAL INDEX OF INGREDIENTS

# BIOGRAPHIES

**Cinzia Trenchi** naturopath, journalist, and freelance photographer, specializes in food and enogastronomic tourism. She contributes to several cookbooks published both in Italy and abroad. A passionate cook, she collaborates with Italian magazines for feature stories about regional specialties, tradition, macrobiotics, and natural cooking, providing texts and photographs and offering recipes of her own creation. A curious traveler, she personally experiences local traditions and provides new interpretations for these. She creates cookbooks proposing original diets, offering unusual food combinations, and always keeping in mind the nutritional characteristics of foods, for the purpose of achieving greater balance at the table.

**Fabio Petroni**, since his studies in photography, has worked with some of the most talented professionals in the industry. His career path has led him to specializing in portraits and still lifes. He works with leading advertising agencies and has authored numerous campaigns of worldwide renown. He personally handles the images of certain major Italian brands. For White Star he has published *Horses. Masters portraits* (2010), *Mutt's life!* (2011), *Cocktails* (2012), *Roses* (2012), and *Super Cats* (2012).

**Enzo Monaco**, journalist and Calabrian gastronome, is a firm believer in the importance and role of the chili pepper in the Mediterranean diet, with over 30 years dedicated to study, research, and promotional initiatives regarding the Capsicum. In 1992, he created the "Peperoncino Festival," an annual event taking place at Diamante (Calabria). In 1994, he founded the Italian Chili Pepper Academy, a nonprofit organization that researches and promotes the culture of the chili pepper. In 2010 he created the Calabria Capsicum, an experimental center for cultivation of the chili pepper. Since 2012 he has directed the Università del Gusto (University of Taste).

**Mario Dadomo** is director of the Azienda Agraria Sperimentale Stuard and consultant for regional experimentation regarding industrial tomatoes and onions. He is a member of the International Society of Horticultural Science (ISHS). Author of more than 100 publications of scientific, technical, and popularizing character, he has participated in numerous conferences and seminars and has been a speaker at the International ISHS Symposium regarding the industrial tomato (Sorrento, 1993, and Pamplona, 1998).

THE AUTHOR AND THE PUBLISHER WISH TO THANK:

ENZO MONACO, PRESIDENT OF THE ITALIAN CHILI PEPPER ACADEMY
WWW.PEPERONCINO.ORG

MARIO DADOMO, AZIENDA AGRARIA SPERIMENTALE STUARD
WWW.STUARD.IT

ENZO NICOLELLO - GARDEN DESIGN
WWW.CASCINAMOLINOTORRINE.COM

FRANCESCA BAGNASCHI - FOOD STYLIST

HIGH-TECH MILANO, FOR SUPPLY OF PLATES AND ACCESSORIES
WWW.HIGH-TECHMILANO.COM

**WHITE STAR PUBLISHERS**

WS White Star Publishers® is a registered trademark
property of Edizioni White Star s.r.l.

© 2013 Edizioni White Star s.r.l.
Via M. Germano, 10
13100 Vercelli, Italy
www.whitestar.it

Translation: John Venerella and Salvatore Ciolfi
Editing: Deb Golden

ISBN 978-88-544-0649-0
1 2 3 4 5 6   17 16 15 14 13

Printed in China